A SPIRIT-FILLED CLASSIC

Smith
Wigglesworth

Only
Believe

Edited by Wayne E. Warner

Bridge-Logos

Alachua, Florida 32615

Bridge-Logos

Alachua, Florida 32615 USA

Smith Wigglesworth: Only Believe

Edited by Wayne Warner

Printed in the United States of America.

Library of Congress Catalog Card Number: 2006932777

International Standard Book Number 978-0-88270-003-8

Scripture quotations are taken from the *King James Version* of the Bible.

Photo credits: p. xxviii-xxxv—Flower Pentecostal Heritage Center

G616.318.B.m804.35230

Dedication

I dedicate this devotional work
to my brothers and sisters
in appreciation for their love and support:
Lawrence, Ellis, Josephine, Leonard,
Ernest, Helen, Lester, and George.

Acknowledgments

Appreciation goes to Glenn Gohr, who searched through
old periodicals and files for Smith Wigglesworth's sermons,
and to Sandra Kolsky for placing the sermons
on computer disks.

Contents

Preface

Only believe, only believe
All things are possible, only believe
All things are possible, only believe.
— Paul Rader

It is probably safe to say that nobody identified with the above chorus any more than did the English dynamo, Smith Wigglesworth. The chorus and the scriptural principle so permeated his life and ministry that friends and relatives felt it would be an injustice if they did not sing it at his funeral service.

Wigglesworth and faith were inseparable, which prompted people around the world to call him "The Apostle of Faith." A biography his old friend, Stanley H. Frodsham, wrote a year following his death used that nickname as its title.

"Apostle of Faith" was more than just an honorary title. Wigglesworth sought every day through prayer and study of the Bible to increase his faith so he could help hurting people. Donald Gee, a British contemporary, said of his friend, "His favorite and almost his only subject was faith. No matter what the text, we all knew where he would arrive."

"We often hear the remark, 'He's gone,'" the dean of Elim Bible College said of Wigglesworth at his funeral, "but in this case, he has arrived. Brother Wigglesworth was not an ordinary man, but extraordinary, and it was his faith in God that made him so."

A current American evangelist and TV personality, James Robison, said that Wigglesworth had "an expression of childlike faith and spiritual recklessness that confused the enemy, astounded all, and won victories for all eternity."

It seems fitting then that these selected devotional readings from his sermons be titled, **Only Believe**.

It is my hope and prayer that these Wigglesworth adaptations will challenge and inspire you to seek a closer walk with God and that the Holy Spirit will use you in a greater measure.

Wayne Warner

Springfield, Missouri

Meet Smith Wigglesworth

Smith Wigglesworth was born into a poor family in Menston, 10 miles from Bradford, Yorkshire, England, on June 10, 1859, and was converted at eight years of age. Not a naturally gifted speaker and having little formal education, Wigglesworth left the preaching and teaching to others in his early life, preferring rather to get involved in personal evangelism while working at his plumbing trade. He continued this practice even after he and his wife Mary Jane (Polly) founded a mission church in Bradford in 1889.

In 1907, when Wigglesworth was 48, he learned that God was blessing people with the baptism in the Holy Spirit in Sunderland, a northeastern coastal city about 95 miles from Bradford. He, too, experienced the blessing and soon began preaching with new faith, fire, and courage. Shortly after his baptism in the Holy Spirit at All Saints' Anglican church in Sunderland, he wrote a letter to the Vicar and his wife, A.A. and Mary Boddy. Consequently, Boddy published the letter in his **Confidence** magazine—first in November 1907, and again in October 1908. It was also published in tract form.

Because this testimony portrays an exuberant Spirit-filled believer launching into what eventually would become a worldwide ministry, I thought you would like to get a feel of his own heart a century later. He was no longer living in the early 20th century but, as it were, he was living in the times of the Apostles. Moreover, one of his daily goals was to see his faith increase and move away from unbelief. As you read more about Smith Wigglesworth, you will understand how this experience in Sunderland in 1907 would be the key to what happened during his last 40 years.

Testimony of Smith Wigglesworth

"After seven full days of the Glorious Presence of the Glory of God resting upon me, I send you this testimony for the Glory of God. For three months, I have been exercised about the full Pentecost. I had the clear witness of the Baptism of the Holy Spirit fourteen years ago last July [1894], and this brought a marvelous manifestation of God in special gifts to sick ones, and a constant living and seeking to bring others to Jesus.

"But from time to time when reading the Acts of the Apostles, I saw that the signs were not following as I am led to believe ought to be after a real Pentecost, according to Mark 16. The desire increasingly increased in my very inner soul, giving me a holy breathing cry after this clear manifestation. I have visited meetings at London, and Sunderland, and other places, but always knew they were not seeking Pentecost. There seemed a great deal of letter, but very little of the Spirit that would give the hungry and needy a Baptism of Fire such as would burn up distinctions and officiousness and appearance of pride and evidences of social standing.

"Today I am actually living in the Acts of the Apostles' time; I am speaking with new tongues; the Holy Fire of God's Presence fills me till my pen moves to the glory of God; and my whole being is filled with the Presence of the Holy Ghost. Almost am I led to believe that 20 years is not too long to wait for the Holy Anointing of God the Holy Ghost."

Recalling the Blessing

"On Friday, October 25th, we had a special meeting at the Mission Room, Bowland Street, Bradford, and after waiting about two hours, the Presence of God came in a wonderful way and gave me a move as at the beginning. I perfectly well understood the glow and Holy Presence. Others felt this also.

"On Saturday, I and a friend went on to Sunderland to wait for Pentecost at All Saints', at Mr. Boddy's Church. We had heard much about this blessed work and were encouraged, but after arriving at Sunderland, found the enemy very busy discouraging believers. This did not disturb me, because I had gone with an open mind and prayed much to be clearly convinced if there was anything there that did not reveal the Glory of God that I would at once have cleared out and protested against it, but God was with me there.

"But I found the full Presence and Power to restore believers and to heal the sick. My experience is that this does not take place in some kinds of meetings; the reason is that, to a great measure, they do not believe the full Gospel. And it is nothing new to me to find great leaders against the tongues, and I find that, even in these times, 'they cannot enter in because of their unbelief.' I praise God for Pentecost.

"On Sunday morning, October 26th, after waiting much on God, I went to the Salvation Army Meeting, Roker Avenue. God bless the Army. They at once gave me a welcome, and already realizing His Presence in my body, I longed for communion; and when after praying, the Glory of God covered me. I was conscious at the same time of much the experience I believe Daniel had in his 10th chapter. After this, I regained strength to kneel, and continued in this Holy Glow of God all the day, still realizing a mightier work to follow.

"I went to All Saints'—to the Communion Service—and after this was led on to wait in the Spirit, many things taking place in the waiting-meetings that continued to bring me to a hungry feeling for Holy Righteousness.

"At about 11 a.m. Tuesday morning, at All Saints' Vicarage, I asked a sister [Vicar Boddy's wife Mary] to help me to the witness of the Baptism of the Holy Ghost [speaking in tongues, Acts 2:4]. She lay hands on me in the presence of a brother. The fire fell and burned in me till the Holy Spirit clearly revealed absolute purity before God. At this point, she was called out of the room, and during her absence a marvelous revelation took place; my body became full of light and Holy Presence, and in the revelation I saw an empty Cross. And at the same time, the Jesus I loved and adored crowned in the Glory in a Reigning Position. The glorious remembrance of these moments is beyond my expression to give—when I could not find words to express, then an irresistible Power filled me and moved my being till I found to my glorious astonishment I was speaking in other tongues clearly. After this, a burning love for everybody filled my soul.

"I am overjoyed in giving my testimony, praying for those that fight this truth; but I am clearly given to understand that I must come out of every unbelieving element. I am already witness of signs following. Praise Him."

– SMITH WIGGLESWORTH

The Boddys See More Than a Plumber

Wigglesworth was thrilled at his new walk in the Spirit, but he had no idea that within seven years, at age 55, he would be in North America and the start of an unlikely ministry that would attract thousands.

Another essential key to Wigglesworth's new life and changed ministry is the Boddy couple, Alexander and Mary.

What did they see in this Bradford plumber who had heard about the outpouring of the Holy Spirit and had come to Sunderland to see if it was true? There were plenty of critics and doubters concerning what was happening in the church. Was Wigglesworth another one?

Their stations in life could hardly have been more opposite. Alexander, better known as A.A., was the son of an Anglican rector. He himself became a minister, serving the Sunderland congregation from 1884-1922. A world traveler and travel author, Boddy was a member of England's Royal Geographical Society and Russia's Imperial Geographical Society.

Because he was concerned about the spiritual life of his congregation, Boddy investigated the great Wales revival, which began in 1904, and he visited T.B. Barratt and the Pentecostal revival in Norway. Barratt returned the visit to Sunderland in September 1907, which resulted in several receiving the baptism in the Holy Spirit—including the Boddys.

The next month, Wigglesworth put aside his plumbing tools and went to Sunderland. And you have just read his testimony of the spiritual experience that took place during the few days he spent in that city.

Maybe the Boddy couple had a witness of the Holy Spirit that this Bradford plumber was a diamond in the rough, that the Lord would use him as He did some rough fishermen and a tax collector 1,900 years earlier. If this had been the case, they would have known for certain that God is no respecter of persons. And in years that were to come, they would know Wigglesworth as an intense worshiper of the

King of kings and as an evangelist who stirred churches and cities wherever he went.

Forty Years of Preaching Begin

After the Sunderland experience, word soon got around that the Bradford plumber was on fire, and people were lining up to see him burn. Eventually, he received numerous invitations to preach, and he felt that God was leading him into full-time evangelism. Plumbing was forgotten as he plunged into reaching the lost and hurting. Some of these preaching points included cities throughout the British Isles, the Continent, Scandinavian countries, North America, Australia, New Zealand, Sri Lanka, and South Africa.

For the next forty years, he taught and preached that Jesus could save sinners, sanctify believers, heal the sick, deliver from demons, baptize in the Holy Spirit, and prepare believers for an eternal home. He underscored his theme that believers could have a dynamic relationship with God in the here and now. Wigglesworth's name became known everywhere he went because of his contagious faith, widely circulated sermons published in books and magazines, and often controversial statements and actions.

A Double-Portion

But before he would reach needy people around the world and gain notoriety, sorrows shook his faith to its foundation. With God's help, however, he weathered them all.

Prior to his Sunderland experience, Wigglesworth's wife Polly was the preacher of the family, and he would give support in their Bradford mission church—being used by the Holy Spirit in a "helps" ministry rather than preaching.

When Wigglesworth returned from his "Damascus Road" experience in Sunderland, Polly had her doubts about his baptism in the Holy Spirit. But when she heard him preach, she knew that something had happened to her husband. She, too, received the baptism in the Holy Spirit along with others in Bradford.

Six years later, during which time Wigglesworth would continue his plumbing business and preaching, Polly died. It shattered Wigglesworth, a man who believed all things were possible. He told a friend, "After [Polly's] funeral, I went back and lay on her grave. I wanted to die there." But God told him to leave the grave, Wigglesworth said. The grieving man bargained with God. "I told Him that if he would give me a double-portion of the Spirit—my wife's and my own—I would go and preach the Gospel."

Later he would give credit for his success to Polly, saying, "All that I am under God, I owe to my precious wife." Now at her death, he asked God to pass Polly's portion of the Spirit to him. A double-portion.

Friends and acquaintances knew it was a double-portion of the Spirit that took him around the world, but he went alone unless his daughter Alice traveled with him. He admitted that he would often weep because of his loneliness and his memories of Polly.

Polly's death was only the first of two major tragedies in his early Spirit-filled walk. In 1915, following his first evangelistic trip to North America, Wigglesworth suffered the loss of his 19-year-old son George.

No doubt, his close walk with God took him through this double loss of his wife and son.

Sorrow Turns to Faith in Action

In challenging his hearers to put faith in action, Wigglesworth thundered, "If you do not venture, you remain ordinary as long as you live. If you dare the impossible, then God will abundantly do far above all you ask or think."

At times, he was accused of insensitivity because of his rough treatment of those seeking his prayers. Wigglesworth explained that he was angry at the devil and sometimes the sick got in the way. But he was not insensitive. Friends saw the private side of Wigglesworth—the man who would weep and pray over prayer requests that reached him from around the world. And if he offended anyone, he would make certain he reached that person with a genuine apology.

Firmly convinced that a supernatural power was essential to combat demons and sickness, Wigglesworth said, "It is not sufficient just to have a touch or to have a desire. There is only one thing that will meet the needs of people today. And that is to be immersed in the life of God. He will take you and fill you with His Spirit until you eat or drink or whatever you do, it shall be all for the glory of God."

Oblivious to those around him, Wigglesworth practiced his explosive faith in railroad cars as trains sped across the countryside, in ships crossing the English Channel and oceans, as he walked along busy city streets, in crowd-filled parks, as well as in public meetings in church buildings, open air, and in sweltering tents. As a result, for 40 years he attracted people to Christ wherever he went.

A.A. Boddy was not the only Anglican vicar who appreciated Wigglesworth's ministry. W.H. Stuart-Fox, whose son had been healed under Wigglesworth's ministry, invited him for a 10-day crusade in a tent near St. Saviour's Church in north London. Then he wrote a glowing report for the July 1928 British Assemblies of God magazine, ***Redemption Tidings***. "That stalwart of evangelism which sets forth Christ as an all-sufficient Saviour for every need of body as well as soul, Mr. Smith Wigglesworth, spent ten busy days at St. Saviour's Church. The great truths so faithfully proclaimed of a full redemption for body, soul, and spirit through the atonement came with extraordinary freshness to the hungry crowds, which day by day filled the tent till it overflowed. One of the striking features of the mission was the large number of men, old and young, which came forward to confess Christ, while there were many cases of healing."

Other churches and pastors called on his services, which leads us to an incident in a Pastor Ruft's church. There, a blind man showed up and said he would not leave until he was healed. Most would panic. Not Wigglesworth. He told the pastor, "Brother Ruft, this is the opportunity of our lives."

Hurrying to the mission, they prayed for the determined man. The writer of Wigglesworth's first biography, Stanley Frodsham, reported that the healed man rushed home to see his father and mother.

That evening when the service was scheduled to begin, the healed man was there, telling everyone about his healing. Like the man in the Bible, he could say, "Once I was blind, but now I see."

Wigglesworth did not preach that night, he said, because the former blind man completely took the meeting out of his hands. "We surely had a wonderful time, for God gave us a great visitation," he added.

A Legacy of Healing, Inspiration, and Miracles

Among the several countries in which Wigglesworth held highly successful meetings were Norway and Sweden in the 1920s. In Oslo, the Norwegian Pentecostal pioneer, T.B. Barratt, tried to explain Wigglesworth's success. "God has mightily used him … the chief reason is the fact that he is filled with the Holy Ghost, and has a faith that never gives way to the wiles of the devil, but faces all opposition in a firm, but beautiful spirit that inspires others and gives them a real lift on the upward line."

An example of the opposition came in Switzerland where he was jailed twice for praying for the sick. Laws and ordinances in other countries often cramped his style. In Sweden, for example, city officials told him he could not lay hands on the sick, his usual practice based on the Bible: "Is any sick among you? Let him call for the elders of the church; and let them pray over him, anointing him with oil in the name of the Lord. And the prayer of faith shall save the sick, and the Lord shall raise him up; and if he have committed sins, they shall be forgiven him" (James 5:14, 15). So, he prayed for the crowd, urging them to lay hands on their own illness.

Regrettably, Wigglesworth has been given credit for miracles far beyond his own claims. Because he never claimed some of the healings and miracles that have circulated in recent years, it seems obvious that he has become a victim of exaggeration. If it were possible for him to return today, he no doubt would put a damper on several undocumented stories, and say that God cannot bless exaggerations. The healings that did happen in some of his meetings did not need the help of exaggerations.

Many people sought out Wigglesworth to be healed or discover his spiritual secrets. One of these was the American Pentecostal minister, Lester Sumrall. In the late 1930s, Sumrall had his opportunity when he spent two years in England, just before the outbreak of World War II.

Wigglesworth invited Sumrall to his home in Bradford, but the visit was not quite as Sumrall expected. "I thought I had come to talk, but he read to me a half hour from the Bible," Sumrall wrote in **Pioneers of Faith**. Then Wigglesworth told him that it was time to pray, which lasted another half hour.

"He laid hands on me and prayed, 'God, bless him! God, bless him!' My body was becoming weary. I was glad when he got through." But then Wigglesworth read to Sumrall again for a half hour, following this with another 30-minute prayer.

"Finally," Sumrall recalled, "he got up from his knees and began to tell beautiful stories of how God had healed this disease and that condition. I sat there weeping, absolutely overwhelmed."

Sumrall returned to the old warrior's home in Bradford about every ten days for the two years he remained in England. "I received life in that house," he wrote some 60 years later. "My faith began to mount up strong in the presence of this man. We became good friends."

Sumrall, who had interacted with many Christian leaders by that time, described Wigglesworth as "an extremely remarkable man, totally sold out to God." Wigglesworth had his own expression for the Spirit-led walk. He called it, "to be immersed in the life of God."

Like every human, Wigglesworth had his faults and critics, even among his Pentecostal peers. His old friend Donald Gee summed up his life when he wrote, "Whatever his faults, Smith Wigglesworth was a man of God."

A trait often seen in Wigglesworth as a man of God was his generosity. Royalties from his books went to missions in the Congo. Stanley Frodsham, his biographer for **Apostle of Faith**, told about Wigglesworth taking him to a Springfield, Missouri, clothing store, and buying him a new suit. Frodsham never forgot that act of kindness.

Two Prophesies

As a man of God, Wigglesworth prophesied over two men who made a difference in their world. The first involved a 15-year-old American boy by the name of Kenneth Ware. Ware's father was killed during World War I, so his mother moved back to her native Switzerland. Kenneth grew up a neglected child and stuttered badly. One day, he was running down a street in Vevey, Switzerland, when a man called to him.

What happened next would change his life.

"Come here, boy!" Wigglesworth commanded. "Put out your tongue!"

At the time, Ware said he thought it could be an American doctor, maybe one his mother knew. He then learned that it was Wigglesworth who was conducting meetings there. Wigglesworth took hold of Ware's tongue and proclaimed, "Lad, this tongue will preach the Gospel."

Although Ware was not converted until a year later, his stuttering stopped as Wigglesworth spoke. Later, he felt called to preach and became a dedicated missionary to France, risking his life to minister to persecuted Jews during World War II. He also reached out to Muslims, Gypsies, and other needy people.

And it all began when a stranger told him to stick out his tongue and prophesied.

The second prophecy happened in South Africa where Wigglesworth was ministering in 1936, and it involved a 30-year-old minister of the Apostolic Faith Mission, which was founded by another well-known evangelist, John Lake. The young minister, David du Plessis, later told how Wigglesworth began to prophesy that a greater revival than anything they had seen would happen, and Du Plessis would have a prominent part.

Du Plessis was shocked as Wigglesworth continued to speak to him about the future when non-Pentecostal denominations and leaders would accept the baptism in the Holy Spirit. Wigglesworth closed his prophecy, which Du Plessis recounts in his 1977 book, *A Man Called Mr. Pentecost*:

"All he requires of you is that you be humble and faithful under all circumstances."

Wigglesworth did not live to see that revival, which is generally referred to as the Charismatic Movement and which began about 1960, but du Plessis became a prominent part as Wigglesworth prophesied in 1936.

As David du Plessis saw doors open from Princeton to the Vatican for him and his once despised Pentecostal message, he never forgot the anointed words from the Yorkshire plumber that day in South Africa.

Extraordinary, Even in Death

When Wigglesworth died in 1947 at the age of 88, an English acquaintance, Freida Birney, wrote about an amazing incident in a letter to Stanley Frodsham, editor of the U.S. *Pentecostal Evangel*. Frodsham published it in the August 2, 1947, issue.

As the story goes, Mrs. Birney had attended a 1932 missionary meeting, which Wigglesworth conducted. In one of the meetings, she recalled, Wigglesworth stated that he had asked the Lord for fifteen more years. And just as the Lord extended King Hezekiah's life by fifteen years, He extended Wigglesworth's. Mrs. Birney added, "It is remarkable that it was fifteen years to the very week that the Lord took him home."

Wigglesworth never was one to do anything ordinary— even in dying.

Now, nearly sixty years after his death, Smith Wigglesworth still inspires others through his faith-building sermons and inspirational writings such as you will read in this book.

Wigglesworth would often say that nobody would catch him without his Bible. Here he is in a familiar pose.

James and Alice Wigglesworth Salter, Smith Wigglesworth's daughter and son-in-law. They were missionaries to the Congo but would often travel with Wigglesworth on his overseas trips.

Wigglesworth often preached at North American camp meetings. Here he is with his daughter Alice in Eureka Springs, Arkansas, in the 1920s.

YOU SIMPLY MUST HEAR
Evangelist
Smith Wigglesworth
OF ENGLAND

EVANGELISTIC AND
DIVINE HEALING CAMPAIGN

at the

First
Pentecostal
Church

31st Street, near Grove

January 2
—to—

January 15

Evangelist Smith Wigglesworth

WEEK DAYS—10:30 A. M. and 7:45 P. M. except Mondays and
Saturdays. Saturdays at 7:45 P. M.

SUNDAYS—11:00 A. M., 3:00 and 7:15 P. M.

THE SICK PRAYED FOR AT EACH SERVICE

A RARE OPPORTUNITY TO HEAR A WORLD EVANGELIST

An advertisement for meetings in Oakland, California, in 1930.

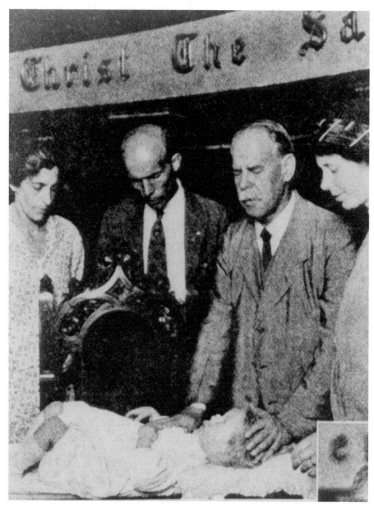

Wigglesworth and others praying for a child at Aimee Semple McPherson's Angelus Temple, Los Angeles, about 1929. Published in McPherson's **Bridal Call** magazine.

Years and again Soloman was sent out. A last time I spoke to Soloman, and he had scarcely left the door before he came running into the room crying that clouds were gathering rapidly.

It was easy to pray now and our hearts went out in praise and victory. The great drops began to patter on the roof. Then the downpour came in earnest. Not waiting for it to cease, the chiefs and natives went shouting and crying out, 'The Lord God, He is the Great Chief: the Lord God, He is the God above all Gods'. "

1921

IN THE SERVICE OF
THE KING

"If God be for us." who can be against us? We are glad to report victory for our Lord and Saviour in Atwater. The past summer has been rich with many blessings from the Lord. A number have been saved and baptized in the Holy Spirit. Twenty-two have been baptized in water.

The church building has been completed inside and out, and its time all paid for, so we rejoice in what the Lord has done in our midst. The fellowship and unity of the saints has remained unbroken. We also have had the opportunity of having street meetings, where large numbers of people have been listening to the story that never grows old. The Lord has magnified His own words and we are encouraged to press on for greater opportunities are ahead.

— Eric M. Johnson
January 1925

AT GLAD TIDINGS TEMPLE
1451 Ellis Street, San Francisco, Calif.

OLD TIME PENTECOSTAL REVIVAL

Evangelist
Smith
Wigglesworth
of England

December 8
to
December 22
Inclusive

Evangelist Smith Wigglesworth

WEEK DAYS—10:30 A. M. and 7:45 P. M.
SUNDAYS—11:00 A. M., 3:00 and 7:15 P. M.

All Are Invited to Attend These Special Meetings
The Sick Prayed for at Each Service

Apply Early and We Will Arrange Accommodation
for You

23

A 1920s advertisement for a meeting at Glad Tidings Temple in San Francisco.

*Above: Wigglesworth
standing at the ruins
of a castle in England.*

Wigglesworth Leak-Proof Anointing Bottle

A very neat, compact bottle of convenient size. Sure to please.

Guaranteed
Leak-Proof

Illustration actual
size

Price $1.00
Postpaid

(We are the sole agents in this country)

The "Ideal Anointing Vial for Pastors and Evangelists!

Address all Mail Orders to Glad Tidings Book Room, 1441 Ellis Street, San Francisco, Calif.

*Glad Tidings Temple,
San Francisco, distributed
Wigglesworth's anointing oil
bottle, which was designed
for use in churches or while
visiting the sick (based on
James 5:14).*

A well-known portrait of Wigglesworth.

Artist Doug Latta's portrait made from a Wigglesworth photograph, which hung in the PTL Heritage Village.

Only Believe

Fear not, little flock, from the cross to the throne,

From death into life He went for His own;

All power in earth, all power above,

Is given to Him for the flock of His love.

Chorus: Only believe, only believe;

All things are possible, only believe;

Only believe, only believe;

All things are possible, only believe.

Fear not, little flock, He goeth ahead,

Your Shepherd selecteth the path you must tread;

The waters of Marah He'll sweeten for thee,

He drank all the bitter in Gethsemane.

Fear not, little flock, whatever your lot,

He enters all rooms, "the doors being shut;"

He never forsakes, He never is gone,

So, count on His presence in darkness and dawn.

— Paul Rader

–1–

Ready for Everything

While he [Jesus] yet spake, there came from the ruler of the
synagogue's house certain which said, Thy daughter is dead; why
troublest thou the Master any further? As soon as Jesus heard the
word that was spoken, he saith unto the ruler of the synagogue,
"Be not afraid, only believe" (Mark 5:35, 36).

Praise the Lord! Praise the Lord! Praise the Lord!
Only believe! Only believe!
All things are possible,
Only believe.

There is something very remarkable about this chorus. God
wants to impress it so deeply on our hearts today that we may
get so engrossed in this divine truth that we will know all things
are possible if we only believe! Then, he can get in us and he
can get out of us, for others, that which would otherwise never
be possible.

Oh, for this truth to lay hold of us today, the truth that God comes
to us afresh and says, "Only believe!" Beloved, let me tell you, this
chorus will help you. Beloved, I trust today the Lord will give me
something to make you ready for everything that will come into
your life, so that you will not be behind time, but in the place God
has designed for you.

૨૦ ૨૦ ૨૦

−2−

Praying in the Holy Spirit

I want to tell you of an amazing incident that illustrates the power in praying in the Holy Spirit.

William Burton is associated with my son-in-law, James Salter, in Africa. When they were going into the Congo [now Zaire] to begin the ministry, one of their men died; and then Burton was laid low with the fever. He seemed dead, and the party went on broken-heartedly. But looking around, they saw him coming on just as lively as though he had never had a touch of fever.

"What has happened?" they shouted. "Tell us!" And he said, "From my head right down, there came a warmth of life through my body, and here I am perfectly well."

Afterwards, when Burton was in a meeting in England, a woman asked him if he kept a diary. When he answered that he did, she asked him to look on a certain date, which she gave to him.

While he was looking it up, she went on, "I saw you lying as one dead, and I was broken down before God in your behalf and was praying for you when the Spirit filled me and there I was speaking in an unknown tongue. And when I got through, I saw you looking perfectly well." Burton found in his diary that it was the very hour of his recovery.

What we need is more of the Holy Spirit. Oh, let it be no longer we, but the Spirit who prays!

-3-

Acting in the Name of Jesus

On an ocean vessel one day, someone asked me if I would sing during the evening entertainment. I agreed, and at my request, they put me on the list just before the dance.

I longed for my turn to come because there had been a minister aboard who had tried to sing and entertain them, and it seemed so out of place. When my turn came, I sang: "If I Could Only Tell Him as I Know Him."

When I got through, some of the people—including a minister—said I had spoiled the dance. I looked at it as my opportunity, and I took it for the Lord. You see, I was in the drama of life acting in the Name of Jesus. Glory to God!

When the preacher arrived in India, he wrote an article for his periodical and sent it to England. He said, "I did not seem to have any chance to preach the Gospel, but there was a plumber on board who seemed to have plenty of opportunities to preach to everybody, and he said things to me that remain. He told me that the Acts of the Apostles was only written because they acted."

And so that experience opened the door and got me in the place that I could speak anytime during the rest of the voyage.

⁂ ⁂ ⁂

–4–

Victory through Jesus Christ

God expects each believer to put on the whole armor he has provided (Ephesians 6:10-20), and he wants us to be covered with his Spirit and to grow in grace and the knowledge of him. Oh, what God has laid up for us and what we may receive through the name of Jesus! Oh, the value of the Name, the power of the Name; the very name of Jesus brings help from heaven, and the very Name of Jesus can bind evil powers and subdue all things unto himself. Thank God for victory through our Lord Jesus Christ. To save us, he endured the Cross, despising the shame.

How beautiful it is to say with our entire being, "I will be obedient unto God." Oh, he is lovely! He is beautiful! I do not remember ever coming to him when he denied me anything. He has never turned me away empty. He is such a wonderful Savior, such a Friend that we can depend upon with assurance and rest and complete confidence. He can roll away every burden.

Wherever you are, whatever your situation, think of him as the exhaustless Savior, the everlasting Friend, one who knows all things, one who is able to help and deliver us. When we have such a Source as this, we can stretch out our hands and take all that we need from him.

꩜ ꩜ ꩜

—5—

Faith Cometh by Hearing

And Jesus entered into Jerusalem, and into the temple;
and when he had looked round about upon all things, and now the
eventide was come, he went out unto Bethany with the twelve. And
on the morrow, when they were come from Bethany he was hungry …
and seeing a ×g tree afar off having leaves he came, if haply he might
×nd any thing thereon; and when he came to it, he found nothing but
leaves; for the time of ×gs was not yet. And Jesus answered and said
unto it, "No man eat fruit of thee hereafter forever." And his disciples
heard it (Mark 11:11-14).

The fig tree dried up from the roots. We may think we have faith in God, but we must not doubt in our hearts. "What things soever ye desire, when ye pray, believe that ye receive them, and ye shall have them" (Mark 11:24). This is a very wonderful word on faith, a subject you obviously are interested in pursuing.

You must realize that your inactivity must be brought to a place of victory. Inactivity—that which wavers, that which hesitates, that which fears instead of having faith, that closes up everything because it doubts instead of believing God.

What is faith? Faith is the living principle of the Word of God. It is life, it produces life, and it changes life. God wants us to feed on the Book, the living Word, the precious Word of God. "Faith cometh by hearing, and hearing by the Word of God" (Romans 10:17).

꒰ ꒰ ꒰

−6−

ing More Like Jesus

A ll the wonderful things that Jesus did were done that people
might be changed and made like unto himself. He went about
his Father's business and was eaten up with the zeal of his house.
Oh, to be like him in thought, act, and plan!

I am beginning to understand 1 John 3:2. "Beloved, now are we
the sons of God, and it doth not yet appear, what we shall be:
but we know that, when he shall appear we shall be like him;
for we shall see him as he is." As I feed on the Word of God, my
whole body will be changed by the process of the power of the
Son of God. "But if the Spirit of him that raised up Jesus from the
dead dwell in you, he that raised up Christ from the dead shall
also quicken your mortal bodies by his Spirit that dwelleth in you"
(Romans 8:11).

The Lord dwells in a humble and contrite heart, and makes his
way into the dry places, so if you open up to him, he will flood
you with his life; but remember that a little bit of sin will spoil a
whole life. You can never cleanse sin; you can never purify sin;
you can never be strong while in sin; you will never have a vision
while in sin. Revelation stops when sin comes in. The human
spirit must come to an end, but the spirit of Christ must be alive
and active. You must die to the human spirit, and then God will
quicken your mortal body and make it alive. "Without holiness,
no man shall see God."

ॐ ॐ ॐ

−7−

Living by Faith

Today we have a wonderful subject. What is it? Faith. Faith is an inward operation of that divine power which dwells in the contrite heart, and which has power to lay hold of the things not seen. Faith is a divine act. Faith is God in the soul. God operates by his Son, and transforms the natural into the supernatural. Faith is active, never dormant; faith lays hold; faith is the hand of God; faith is the power of God; faith never fears; faith lives amid the greatest conflict; faith is always active; faith moves even things that cannot be moved. God fills us with his divine power, and sin is dethroned. "The just shall live by faith." You cannot live by faith until you are just (righteous). You cannot live by faith if you are unholy or dishonest.

The Lord was looking for fruit when he cursed the tree in Mark 11:11-15. He found "nothing but leaves." There are thousands of people like that. They dress up like Christians, but it is all leaves. "Herein is My Father glorified, that ye bear much fruit" (John 15:8). He has no way in which to get fruit except through us. We are not to be ordinary people. To be saved is to be an extraordinary person—an exposition of God.

When Jesus was talking about the new life, he said, "Except a man be born of God, he cannot see the kingdom of God. That which is born of the flesh is flesh; and that which is born of the Spirit is Spirit" (John 3:3, 6).

-8-

The Truth Shall Make You Free

There are none so deaf as those who will not hear, and none so blind as those who will not see. But if God has given you ears and eyes, he wants you to hear and see.

What does God want me to know? "And ye shall know the truth, and the truth shall make you free" (John 5:32).

Do you remember what Jesus asked about the spiritual strength of John the Baptist after John had been thrown into prison? You will find this narrative beginning in Matthew 11:7. "As they departed, Jesus began to say unto the multitudes concerning John, 'What went ye out into the wilderness to see? A reed shaken with the wind?'"

Did you ever see a man of God like a reed? If ever you did, I should say he was only an imitator. Has God ever made a man to be a reed, or to be like smoking flax? No. God wants to make men as flames of fire. God wants to make men strong in the Lord and in the power of his might.

Therefore, beloved, if you will hear the truth of the Gospel, you will see that God has made provision for you to be strong, to be on fire, to be as though you were quickened from the dead, as those who have seen the King, as those who have a resurrection touch.

We know we are the sons of God with power as we believe his Word and stand in the truth of his Word.

–9–

Divine Power in Human Vessels

Divine life does not belong to this world, but to the kingdom of heaven, and the kingdom of heaven is within you. God wants to purify our minds until we can bear all things, believe all things, hope for all things, and endure all things (1 Corinthians 13:7). God dwells in you, but you cannot have this divine power until you live and walk in the Holy Ghost, until the power of the new life is greater than the old life.

God wants us to move mountains, and anything that appears to be a mountain can be moved. The mountains of difficulty, the mountains of perplexity, the mountains of depression or depravity. Things that have bound you for years. Sometimes things appear as though they could not be moved, but believe in your heart, stand on the Word of God, and God's Word will never be defeated.

Notice again this Scripture: "What things soever ye desire, when ye pray, believe that ye receive them, and ye shall have them" (Mark 11:24).

First, believe that ye receive them, and ye shall have them. That is the difficulty with people. They say, "Well, if I could feel I have it, I would know I have it." But you must believe it, and then the feeling will come; you must believe it because of the Word of God. God wants to work in you a real heart faith. I want you to know that God has a real remedy for all your ailments. There is power in his Word to set everybody free.

–10–

A New Commandment

It is always a very blessed time for believers to gather for communion in remembrance of the Lord. Jesus said, "This do in remembrance of me."

When we gather to commemorate our Lord's wonderful death, victory, and triumph, and look forward to the "glorious hope," we need to get rid of our religion. It has been "religion" at all times that has slain and destroyed that which was good. Sad as it is to say, when Satan entered into Judas, the only people that the devil could speak to through Judas were the priests. They conspired to get him to betray Jesus, and the devil took money from these priests to put Jesus to death.

Now, it is a very serious thing, for we must clearly understand whether we are of the right spirit or not, for no man can be of the Spirit of Christ and persecute another. No man can have the true Spirit of Jesus and slay his brother, and no man can follow the Lord Jesus and have enmity in his heart. You cannot have Jesus and have bitterness and hatred, and persecute the believer.

Do you want a new commandment, one that will change your life and that of others? You will find it in John 13:34, 35: "A new commandment I give unto you, that ye love one another, as I have loved you, that ye also love one another. By this shall all men know that ye are my disciples, if ye have love one to another."

$-11-$

Having the Right Spirit

It is possible for us, if we are not careful, to have within us an evil spirit of unbelief, and even in our best state, it is possible for us to have enmity unless we are perfectly dead and let the life of the Lord lead us.

I want to remind you of the time Jesus wanted to pass through a certain place on his way to Jerusalem. Because he would not stop and preach to them concerning the kingdom, the people refused to allow him to go through their section of the country. And the disciples with Jesus said to him, "Wilt thou that we command fire to come down from heaven, and consume them, even as Elias did?" (Luke 9:54). But Jesus turned and said, "Ye know not what manner of spirit ye are of" (verse 55).

There they were, following Jesus and with him all the time, but Jesus rebuked that spirit. I pray to God that we may come to a place that our knowledge of Jesus is pure love, and pure love to Jesus is death to self on all lines—body, soul, and spirit. I believe that if we are in the will of God, we will be perfectly directed at all times. And if we would know anything about the mighty works of Christ, we shall have to follow what Jesus said.

> *All to Jesus I surrender,*
> *All to Him I freely give;*
> *I will ever love and trust Him,*
> *In His presence daily live.*
> *- Judson W. Van de Venter*

꙳ ꙳ ꙳

–12–

Obedience Brings Victory

Many things happened in the lives of the apostles to show them that the Lord Jesus had power over all flesh. In regard to paying tribute, Jesus said to Peter, "We are free, we can enter the city without paying tribute; nevertheless, we will pay."

I like that thought, that Jesus was righteous on all lines. It helps me a great deal. Then Jesus told Peter to do a very hard thing. He said, "Go thou to the sea, and cast a hook, and take up the fish that first cometh up; and when thou hast opened his mouth, thou shalt find a piece of money; that take and give unto them for me and thee" (Matthew 17:27).

No doubt, many things were in Peter's mind that day, but thank God, there was one fish, and Peter obeyed. Sometimes to obey in blindness brings the victory. Sometimes when perplexities arise in your mind, obedience means God works out the problem.

Peter cast the hook into the sea, and it would have been amazing if you could have seen the disturbance the other fish made to move out of the way, all except the right one. God wanted one among the millions of fish.

God may put his hand upon you in the midst of millions of people. But if he speaks to you, what he says will be appointed.

-13-

The Life of the Spirit

I was taken to see a young woman who was very ill. The young man who showed me the way said, "I am afraid we shall not be able to do much here because of her mother; and the doctors are coming." I said, "This is the reason God brought me here." When I prayed, the young woman was instantly healed by the power of God. After that, crowds came, and I ministered to the sick among them for two hours. God the Holy Spirit tells us in our hearts today, that it is only he who can do it.

The secret for the future is living and moving in the power of the Holy Spirit. One thing I rejoice in is that there need not be an hour or a moment when we do not know that the Holy Spirit is upon us.

Oh, this glorious life in God is beyond expression. It is God manifest in the flesh. Oh, this glorious unction of the Holy Spirit—that we move by the Spirit. He should be our continual life. The inward man receives the Holy Spirit instantly with great joy and blessedness. He cannot express it. Then the power of the Spirit, this breath of God, takes of the things of Jesus and sends forth as a river the utterances of the Spirit.

The Holy Spirit has the last thoughts on things that God wants to give. Glory to God for the Holy Spirit! We must see that we live in the place where we say, "What wilt thou have me to do?" and are in the place where he can work in us to make known the mystery of his will and to do of his good pleasure (Ephesians 1:9).

⟞⟝ ⟞⟝ ⟞⟝

-14-

When God Is in Control

On one occasion, Jesus told the disciples that when they went into the city, they would see a man bearing a pitcher of water. They should follow him. It was not customary in the East for men to carry anything on their heads. Women always did the carrying.

When they found the man with the pitcher, they asked him, "Where is the guest chamber?"

"How strange it is that you should ask," he replied, "I have been preparing it, wondering who wanted it."

It is marvelous that when God is leading, everything works perfectly into the plan. He was arranging everything. You think he cannot do that for you today? For people who have been in perplexities for days and days, he knows how to deliver them out of trouble. He can be with you in your darkest hour. He can make all things work together for good to them that love God (Romans 8:28). He has a way of arranging his plan; and when God comes in, you always know it was a day you lived in God. Oh, to live in God!

There is a vast difference between living in God and living in speculation and hope. There is something better than hope; something better than speculation. "The people that do know their God shall be strong and do exploits" (Daniel 11:32).

ॐ ॐ ॐ

−15−

The Hour that Changed the World

There is something that brings believers together. I have experienced God's wonderful drawing power in Europe, South Africa, Australia, New Zealand, Ceylon, Canada, the United States, and many other places. And it is just the same despite language barriers and cultural differences. It is because of a living faith in him. We see this so beautifully displayed during the Lord's last Passover.

"And when the hour was come, he sat down and the twelve apostles with him" (Luke 22:14). "When the hour was come"—that was the most wonderful hour. There never was another hour, never will be another hour like that one. What hour was it? It was an hour of the passing of creation under the Blood. It was an hour of destruction of demon power. It was an hour appointed for life to come out of death. It was an hour when all that had ever lived came under a glorious covering of the Blood. It was an hour when all the world was coming into emancipation by the Blood. It was an hour in history when the world emerged from dark chaos. It was a wonderful hour!

Praise God for that hour! Was it a dark hour? It was a dark hour for him, but a wonderful light dawned for us. It was tremendously dark for the Son of Man, but praise God he came through it.

ॐ ॐ ॐ

–16–

Laughing at Trouble

There are some things in scripture, which move me greatly. I am glad that Jesus was human when he walked this earth. I am glad that Paul was human. I am glad that Daniel was human, and I am also glad that John was human. Why? Because I see that whatever God has done for other men, he can do for me. And I find God has done such wonderful things for other men that I am always on the expectation that these things are possible for me.

One day, a man was preaching, and he said that perhaps Jesus had arranged ahead of time for a colt to be tied and waiting for him. And another preacher said it was quite easy for Jesus to feed all those thousands of people, because the loaves in those days were so tremendously big. But he did not tell his audience that it was a little boy who had the five loaves. Unbelief can be very blind, but faith can see through a stonewall.

Hebrews 11, the "faith" chapter, has two verses to strengthen you today: "Now faith is the substance of things hoped for, the evidence of things not seen" (verse 1); "But without faith it is impossible to please him: for he that cometh to God must believe that he is, and that he is a rewarder of them that diligently seek him" (verse 6).

Faith, when it is moved by the power of God, can laugh when there is trouble.

—17—

The Price of Our Salvation

Think about this wonderful thought. When Jesus approached the crucifixion, he said, "With desire I have desired to eat this Passover with you before I suffer" (Luke 22:15).

Desire? What could be his desire? His desire because of the salvation of the world. His desire because of dethronement of the powers of Satan. His desire because he knew he was going to conquer everything and make free every person who ever lived.

It was a great desire, but what lay between the desire and its fulfillment? Between that moment and the cross lay Gethsemane! Some people say that Jesus died on the cross, and that is perfectly true, but is that the only place? No. Jesus died in Gethsemane. That was a tragic moment! Gethsemane was between him and the cross.

I want you to think about Gethsemane. There alone, and with the tremendous weight, the awful effect of all sin and disease upon his body, he cried out, "If it be possible, let it pass." Oh, could it be! He could only save when he was man, but here like a giant refreshed and coming out of a great chaos of darkness, he comes forth. "To this end I came." It was his purpose to die for the world.

And that includes you and me. Praise God!

꒰꒰ ꒰꒰ ꒰꒰

-18-

A Greater Power in You

I would never have preached the Gospel if I did not know that all the Bible is true. Jesus said, "The devil cometh not, but for to steal, and to kill, and to destroy; I am come that they might have life and that they might have it more abundantly" (John 10:10).

I want you to see the difference between the abundant life of Jesus and the power of Satan. It is only fair and reasonable that I put before you the almightiness of God against the might of Satan. If Satan were almighty, we would all quake. But when we know that Satan in everything is subject to the powers of God, we can become conquerors over him in every situation. We must be strong in the Lord and in the power of his might. There is a power in you that is greater than any power. "Ye are of God, little children, and have overcome them: because greater is he that is in you, than he that is in the world" (1 John 4:4).

I trust, by the help of the Spirit, that you may come into a place of deliverance, a place of holy sanctification where you dare stand against the wiles of the devil, and drive them back, and cast them out. The Lord help us!

–19–

The Baptism in the Spirit Makes the Difference

I believe the Bible from front to back. But it won't have an atom of power for us unless we put that Word into practice. Some people come to me and say, "I have been waiting for the baptism in the Holy Spirit (see Acts 2), and I am having such a struggle. I am having to fight for every inch of it. Isn't it strange?"

No, I believe God is preparing you to help somebody else who is desiring to receive the baptism in the Holy Spirit. In the beginning, I fought the teaching on the baptism in the Holy Spirit, which is accompanied with speaking in tongues. I thought I had experienced the baptism in the Holy Spirit. Then the power of God fell upon me with such ecstasy of joy that I could not express the joy I felt with the natural tongue. The Spirit spoke through me in other tongues.

What did it mean? I knew that I had experienced anointings of joy before, and I had felt joy all the way through my life. But when the fullness came with a high tide, with an overflowing life, I knew that was different from anything else. And I knew that was the baptism, but God had to show me. I trust that through His word, our wonderful Lord will show you, too.

-20-

Wanting to Be Number One

One day the disciples brought to Jesus their argument as to who would be the greatest. Jesus answered, "Whoever will be great among you, let him be your minister; and whosoever will be chief among you, let him be your servant" (Matthew 20:26, 27). Then the Master told them that he was among them as one who serves. He, the noblest, the purest, he was the servant of all!

Hear him speak lovingly, but pointedly: "I am among you as he that serveth. Ye are they which have continued with me in my temptations. And I appoint unto you a kingdom, as my Father hath appointed unto me" (Luke 22:28, 29).

Competing for the higher position is not of God. Exercising lordship over another is not of God. We must learn in our hearts that fellowship, true righteousness, loving one another, and preferring one another must come into the church. Pentecost must outreach everything that ever has been, and we know it will happen if we are willing. But it cannot happen if we are not willing.

We can never be filled with the Holy Spirit so long as there is any human, craving desire for our own will. Selfishness must be destroyed. Jesus was perfect, the end of everything, and God is anxious to make us more like Jesus. It is giving that pays; it is helping that pays; it is loving that pays; it is putting yourself out of the way for another that pays. That is serving for his glory.

−21−

A Daily Consecration

I believe there is a day coming that none of us has yet conceived. This is the testing road. This is the place where your whole body has to be covered with the wings of God. This is the thing for which God is getting you ready, the most wonderful thing your heart can conceive.

How can you get into it? First of all, have you continued with the Lord in his temptations? He had been in trials; he had been in temptation. There is not one of us that is tempted beyond what he was.

If we can be tried, if we can be tempted on any line, Jesus speaks to us as well as his faithful disciples: "Ye are they which have continued with me in my temptations" (Luke 22:28). Have faith and God will keep you pure in the temptation. How shall we reach it? In Matthew 19:28, Jesus said, "Ye which have followed me in the regeneration when the Son of man shall sit in the throne of his glory, ye also shall sit upon twelve thrones, judging the twelve tribes of Israel."

"Follow in regeneration"—every day is a regeneration; every day is a day of advancement; every day is a place of choice. Every day you find yourself in need of fresh consecration. If you are in a place to yield, God moves you in the place of regeneration. That requires a daily consecration.

–22–

When God Says, "Come Out"

For years and years God made me appear to hundreds and thousands of people as a fool. I remember the day when he saved me and when he called me out. If there is a thing God wants to do today, he wants to be as real to you and me as he was to Abraham when he called him out of Ur of the Chaldees (Genesis 12:1).

After I was saved, I joined a very lively group of people who were full of a revival spirit, and it was marvelous how God blessed. Then there came upon them a lukewarmness and indifference, and God said to me as clearly as anything, "Come out." I obeyed and came out. The people said, "We cannot understand you. We need you now, and you are leaving us."

I then felt impressed to join other groups, but one by one, God called me out of them. I obeyed him and went with what they called the "tongues" folks; they received the credit for having further light. I saw God advancing every movement I made, and I can see it even in this Pentecostal work. But unless we see a continued death to sin and self, God will say, "Come out." Unless Pentecost wakes up to shake herself free from all worldly things and comes into a place of the divine-likeness with God, we will hear the voice of God saying, "Come out," and he will have something far better than this.

If you are not on fire, you are not in the place of regeneration. It is only the fire of God that burns up the entanglements of the world.

A time could come when God tells you to come out of the group you are with. Keep in mind, though, he will make a way for you just as he did for me.

-23-

A Place in the Coming Kingdom

When God brought me into a deeper experience with him, he spoke by the Spirit making me know I had to reach the place of absolute yieldedness and cleansing so that there would be nothing left. That meant a clean sweep.

Friend, that was only the beginning, and if you have not made tremendous progress in that holy zeal and power and compassion of God, I can truly say you have backslidden in your heart. The backslider in heart is dead. He has no open vision. The backslider in heart is not seeing the Word of God in a fresh way every day. You can also put it down that a man is a backslider in heart if he is not hated by the world. If you have the applause of the world, you do not have the approval of God.

I do not know whether you will receive it or not, but my heart burns with this message: "Changing in the regeneration" (Matthew 19:28). For in this changing, you will get a place in the kingdom to come where you shall be in authority; that place which God has prepared for us; that place which is beyond all human conception. We can catch a glimpse of that glory, when we read about the angel showing John the wonders of the glorious kingdom (Revelation 19). I wonder if we dare believe for that glorious kingdom.

−24−

The Purpose of Christ's Death

Therefore doth my Father love me, because I lay down my life, that
I might take it again. No man taketh it from me, but I lay it down of
myself. I have power to lay it down, and I have power to take it again.
This commandment have I received of my Father (John 10:17, 18).

It is truly said that by wicked hands Jesus was taken and crucified;
but he had to be willing, for he had all power, and could have
called legions of angels to help him and deliver him from death.
That blessed Christ had purposed to save us and to bring us
into fellowship and oneness. That blessed Savior of God never
looked back, never withheld. He went right through death, that
he might impart unto us this blessed reconciliation between God
and man. So it was the man, Christ Jesus, who is the atonement
for the whole world, the Christ of God, the Son of God. He is
the sinner's friend.

God wants us to know that while he is giving grace and glory, no
good thing will he withhold from the person who walks uprightly.
And that includes health and peace, joy in the Holy Ghost, and
a life in Christ Jesus.

–25–

A "More So" Salvation

Two African men came to our city from the Congo [now Zaire], and my daughter asked if I would show them around. Well, it was a job because they could not speak a word of English. When I was walking with these young men, I kept saying, "Praise the Lord, Amen." After a while they caught on to it; so when I said, "Praise the Lord," they would say, "Amen."

We boarded a car that was full of people, and the young men were at one end and I at the other. They would shout, "Praise the Lord!" and I would respond, "Amen." And we kept it up through the town. They were having a great time.

When they sought the baptism of the Holy Spirit, we had a glorious time. The Holy Spirit fell on them and gave them a new language, so different from their own it was wonderful. They were full of the Spirit and joyful beyond words.

They said, "When we were saved, it was good, very good, but now it is more good, more so!"

O beloved! I know God wants us all to have this "more so" salvation. It is not a measure, but a pressed down measure; and not only a pressed down measure, but a measure shaken together and running over. The baptism of the Spirit is an overflowing cup, praise the Lord!

-26-

The Benefits of Salvation

God wants you to know that he has redemption for you through the Blood of Jesus, which is heaven on earth; which is joy and peace in the Holy Ghost; which is a new birth unto righteousness; which is a change from darkness to light; from the power of Satan unto God. This blessed salvation that God hath made for us through the Blood of his Son is to free you from all the powers of Satan and make you heirs and joint heirs with Christ. Oh, this blessed salvation! Oh, this glorious inheritance that we have in Jesus Christ!

It is a lovely thought to me that three times God rent the heavens with the words, "This is My Beloved Son, in whom I am well pleased." It is true that Christ was born in Bethlehem. It is true that he worked with his father as a carpenter; it is true that he was flesh, like you and me; it is true that God dwelt in that flesh, and manifested his glory so that he was a perfect overcomer. He kept the law and fulfilled his commission, so that he redeemed us by laying down his life. Glory to God!

Jesus was manifested in the flesh; "manifested that he might destroy the power of the devil" (1 John 3:8). What does that mean? It means that he was God's specimen. Oh, it is lovely! I do not know anything more beautiful in the Bible than the specimen of God's power to show you that what he has done for and in Jesus, he could do for and in us.

—27—

Learning Obedience

God can make us overcomers, destroying the power and passion of sin. He can dwell in us by his mighty power and transform our lives till we love righteousness and hate iniquity.

I want you to see that we receive sonship because of his obedience and because of his loyalty. Do not forget, either, what the Scripture says: "Though he were a son, yet learned he obedience by the things he suffered" (Hebrews 5:8). If you turn to the Scripture, you will see that his kindred came and as much as said, "He is possessed by Beelzebub the devil, and is doing his works" (Luke 11:15).

See how he suffered. They reviled him, and they tried to kill him by throwing him over the cliff, but he passed through the midst of the crowd, and as soon as he passed through, he saw a blind man and healed him. Oh, it is lovely!

This power of the new creation, this birth unto righteousness by faith in the atonement, can so transform and change you, that you can be in Christ Jesus and know that the Spirit's power is dominating, controlling, filling you, and making you understand that though you are still in the body, you are governed by the Spirit. What a holy life! What a zeal! What a passion!

❧ ❧ ❧

–28–

Unfeigned Love

There is a constraining power in this blessed Christ of God which makes us know that here is something different from anything in the world. It is called in the Scriptures an "unfeigned love" (1 Corinthians 6:6; 1 Peter 1:22).

Whatever is it? O beloved, he will tell you what it is. It is a denunciation of yourself as the power of Christ lays hold of you so that you could stand fire, water, or anything else in the way of persecution. He loved you when you were yet a sinner, and he seeks your love in return. It is an unfeigned love, a love that can stand ridicule, persecution, and slander because it is an inwrought love by the power of the Holy Spirit making you know that God is changing you by His Spirit from one state of glory to another.

When we were Christ's enemies, he died for us! We can see today that he had chances offered to no other human soul in the world. It was not only the glory of God that was offered him, but the manifestation of a human glory, for they longed in certain circles to make him a king.

If you were told that a country wanted to make you king, you would lose your head and your senses and everything you have. But this blessed Christ of God retired out of the way and went to prayer. He was the greatest King the world will know. He is King of Kings and Lord of Lords. Oh, what a Christ!

꙳ ꙳ ꙳

-29-

Room for Everyone

More than anything else, I like the thought of God calling himself the God of Jacob. I know that if he were only the God of Abraham and Isaac, we might have looked at them and wondered who could reach their standard. But when he says he is the God of Jacob, there is room for everybody. (See Genesis 27-50 for Jacob's spotted history.)

Even after Jacob lived an evil life, God restored him when he willingly returned to Bethel [house of God] and made an altar unto God. This is the promise God made to Jacob there: "Thy name is Jacob: thy name shall not be called any more Jacob, but Israel shall be thy name; and he called his name Israel. And God said unto him, I am God Almighty; be fruitful and multiply; a nation and a company of nations shall be of thee, and kings shall come out of thy loins; And the land which I gave Abraham and Isaac, to thee I will give it, and to thy seed after thee will I give the land" (Genesis 35:10-12).

Hallelujah! Is he your God? He is the God of the sinner.

-30-

Having Our Heart "Fixed" in God

God, through the Apostle Peter, gives us four things for the heart to be fixed in God.

Perfect. In Hebrews 13:21, we read, "Make you perfect in every good work to do his will working in you that which is well pleasing in his sight, through Jesus Christ."

I am perfected as I launch out into God by faith, his Blood covering my sin, his righteousness covering my unrighteousness, his perfection covering my imperfection. I am holy and perfect in him!

Establish. You must be established in the fact that it is his life, not yours. Faith in his Word, faith in his life; you are supplanted by another; you are disconnected from the earth, insulated by faith.

Strengthen. Strengthened in the fact that God is doing the business, not you. You are in the plan, which God is working out.

Tongues with Interpretation: "There is nothing in itself that can bring out that which God designs; what God intends is always a going on to perfection until we are like unto him. It is an establishment of righteousness on his own word."

Settled. What is it to be settled? A knowledge that I am in union with his will, that I am established in the knowledge of it, that day by day I am strengthened. It is an eternal work of righteousness. It is according to your faith. It is as you believe.

࿐ ࿐ ࿐

-31-

Power Over Satan

After Jesus had been transfigured on the mountain, he returned to the valley. There he found a man whose son was in a desperate condition. A devil had taken the boy and thrown him down and bruised him (Matthew 17:14-21; Mark 9:14-29; Luke 9:37-42).

The tenth chapter of John says, "The thief [devil] cometh not, but for to steal, and to kill and to destroy; I am come that they might have life, that they might have it more abundantly" (John 10:10).

The thief cometh, but don't you see that the thief cometh to destroy you? Jesus came to give you life and life more abundant. When he came down among the crowd, the father cried out, "Help me, Lord, help me. Here is my son; the devil taketh him and teareth him till he foams at the mouth, and there he lies prostrate. I brought him to thy disciples, but they could not help me."

Oh, friend, may God strengthen our hands, take away our unbelief. Jesus said, "'O faithless generation, how long shall I be with you? How long shall I suffer you? Bring him unto me.' And they brought him unto him. And Jesus cast out the evil spirit" (Mark 9:19).

Our Lord has come. Bless his Name. Has he come to you? He wants to come to you. He wants to share in your whole life. Nay, verily, he wants to transform your life through his power.

Faith Becomes a Fact

I want you to see that you can receive blessings from God if you will hear the Word. Wherever I go, I meet people who need healing; some want salvation; others want sanctification; and still others want the Baptism of the Spirit. The Word of God says all this came by faith, that it might be by grace. Grace is omnipotence; it is active, benevolent, merciful. It is truth, perfection, and God's inheritance in the soul that can believe.

> *When all around us seems dark as night,*
> *We'll keep on believing and win in the fight.*
> *- Anonymous*

Most people want healing by feeling. It cannot be. Some even want salvation on the same lines, and they say, "Oh, if I could feel I was saved, brother!" It will never come that way.

There are three things, which work together. The first is faith. Faith can always bring a fact, and a fact can always bring joy. So God brings you to His Word—in your own reading or listening to someone else reading it. The Scriptures can make you wise unto salvation, which can open your understanding so you will hear the truth and receive what you need. It's up to you, my friend: God gives you the power to shut the door (reject the Word), and power to open the door (hear and accept the Word).

-33-

True Repentance

Samson has his name recorded in the eleventh chapter of Hebrews as being a man of faith. He was a man who was chosen of God from his mother's womb and who had the power of God coming upon him on certain occasions.

Some people have had the power of the Lord upon them and yet they have lost out. And they know they have lost out. Friend, what about you? God, in his love and kindness, put Samson in Hebrews eleven, the faith chapter. There came a time when, because of Samson's sin, the Philistines were able to cut his hair, tie him with cords, and put out his eyes. As a result, he lost his strength.

He tried to break the cords, but the Philistines had him secure. After his hair grew again, the Philistines wanted him to make sport for them, but he prayed and God answered.

Oh, that we might turn to God and pray this prayer: "O Lord God, remember me, I pray Thee, and strengthen me, I pray Thee, only this once, O God" (Judges 16:28). If you will turn to God with true repentance, he is plenteous in mercy, and he will forgive you. Repentance means getting back to God. When Samson took hold of the pillars upon which the house stood, he pulled the walls down.

God can give you strength, and you can get hold of the posts and he will work through you. No matter what kind of a backslider you have been, there is power in the Blood. "The blood of Jesus Christ his Son cleanseth us from all sin" (1 John 1:7).

-34-

Baptized in the Holy Spirit

Let us read the first four verses from the second chapter of the Acts of the Apostles: "And when the day of Pentecost was fully come, they were all with one accord in one place. And suddenly there came a sound from heaven as of a rushing mighty wind, and it filled all the house where they were sitting. And there appeared unto them cloven tongues like as of fire, and it sat upon each of them. And they were all filled with the Holy Ghost, and began to speak with other tongues, as the Spirit gave them utterance."

What a wonderful divine position God means us all to have, to be filled with the Holy Ghost. There is something so remarkable, so divine, as it were, a great open door into all the treasury of the Most High. As the Spirit comes like rain upon the mown grass, he turns barrenness into greenness and freshness and life.

How glad I am that God baptized me in the Holy Ghost. What a wonderful difference it has made in my life! God has not promised that we should feel very wonderful, but he has promised that if we stand on his Word, he would make his Word real. It is faith first; then it becomes a fact. There are plenty of feelings in the fact, I assure you. And God fills us with His own precious joy. Oh, hallelujah!

-35-

Divine Possibilities

God would have you know that there is a place where he comes to be your assurance and spiritually sustaining power. It will result in spiritual dryness being turned into springs; your barrenness begins to flood; your whole life becomes vitalized by Heaven; Heaven sweeps through you and dwells within and turns everything inside out. And you are absolutely so filled with divine possibilities that you begin to live as a new creation. The Spirit of the living God sweeps through all weaknesses, and he wants to bring us to a great revelation of life. He wants us to be filled with all the fullness of God.

One of the most beautiful pictures we have in the Scriptures is of the Trinity. I want you to see how God unfolded Heaven, and Heaven and earth became the habitation of Trinity. Right on the banks of the Jordan, Trinity was made manifest: the voice of God in the heavens looking at his well-beloved Son coming out of the waters, and there the Spirit was manifested in the shape of a dove (John 1:32).

The dove is the only bird without gall, so timid a creature that at the least thing, it moves and is afraid. No person can be baptized with the Holy Spirit and have bitterness—gall. When the Holy Spirit gets possession, there is a new person entirely—the whole being becomes saturated with divine power. We become a habitation of him who is all light, all revelation, all power, and all love.

Yes, God the Holy Spirit is so manifested within us that it is glorious beyond words.

-36-

How a Rich Man Found True Riches

A certain very successful rich man in London used to pore over his bank book and checks, then scratch his head. He was rich, but he had no peace and didn't know what to do. Walking through his great building, he came to a cheerful boy keeping the door who whistled while he worked. Then the man went back to his office and scratched his head some more. He tried to work, but he could get no peace.

His bank could not help him; his checks, his success could not help him. He had an aching void. He was helpless within. His problem was that he had the world without God.

When he could get no rest, he returned to the happy boy who was keeping the door. Again he found him cheerful and whistling. He asked, "Tell me, what makes you so happy and cheerful?"

"Oh," replied the boy, "I used to be miserable until I went to a little mission and heard about Jesus. Then I was saved and filled with the Holy Spirit. I am always whistling inside; if I am not whistling, I am singing. I am just full!"

The rich man went to a mission service and sat beside the door. The power of God so moved that when the altar call was given, he responded, and God saved him. A few days afterwards, God filled him with the Holy Spirit, he found himself at his desk shouting, "Oh, hallelujah!"

> *I know the Lord, I know the Lord,*
> *I know the Lord's laid His hand on me.*
> *I know the Lord, I know the Lord,*
> *I know the Lord's laid His hand on me.*
> *- Author Unknown*

-37-

The Baptism in the Holy Spirit

The blessed Son of God wants to fill us with such glory till our whole body is aflame with the power of the Holy Spirit. I see there is "much more." Glory to God!

My daughter asked some African boys to tell us the difference between being saved and being filled with the Holy Ghost. "Ah," they said, "when we were saved, it was very good; but when we received the Holy Ghost it was 'more so.'"

After the Holy Ghost comes upon you, you shall have power: God mightily moving within your life. The power of the Holy Ghost will overshadow, inwardly moving you till you know there is a divine plan different from anything that you had in your life before. Has he come? I believe he is going to come today. I am expecting that God shall so manifest his presence and power, that he will show you the necessity of receiving the Holy Ghost.

And that's not all. God will heal you if you need healing. Everything is available now: salvation, sanctification, the fullness of the Holy Ghost, and healing.

God is working mightily by the power of his Spirit, bringing into many lives a fullness of his perfect redemption, until every soul may know that God has all power.

Do you hear his call today?

The Greatest Power in the World

The greatest weakness in the world is unbelief. The greatest power is the faith that worketh by love. Love, mercy, and grace are bound eternally to faith. Fear is the opposite to faith, but there is no fear in love.

The world is filled with fear, torment, remorse, brokenness, but faith and love are sure to overcome. "Who is he that overcometh the world, but he that believeth that Jesus is the Son of God?" (1 John 5:5). God has established the earth and humanity on the lines of faith. As you come into line, fear is cast out, the Word of God comes into operation, and you find bedrock—a solid foundation. All the promises are "yea, and in him amen" to those who believe (2 Corinthians 1:20). When you have faith in Christ, the love of God is so real, you feel you could do anything for Jesus.

They that believe, love. "We love him because he first loved us" (1 John 4:19). When did he love us? When we were in the mire. What did he say? "Thy sins are forgiven thee." Why did he say it? Because he loved us. What for? That he might bring many sons to glory (Hebrews 2:10). His object? That we might be with him forever. "Whatsoever is born of God overcometh the world: and this is the victory that overcometh the world, even our faith" (1 John 5:4).

-39-

An Overcoming Faith

To believe is to overcome. I am heir to all the promises because I believe. A great heritage. I overcome because I believe the truth, and the truth makes me free. Christ is the root and source of our faith; and because he is in what we believe for, it will come to pass. No wavering. This is the principle: he who believes is definite. A definite faith brings a definite experience and a definite utterance.

There is no limit to the power God can bring upon those who cry to him in faith, for he is rich to all who will call upon him. Lay your claim for your children, your families, your co-workers, that many sons may be brought to glory (Hebrews 2:10). As your prayer rests upon the simple principle of faith, nothing shall be impossible to you. The root principle of all this divine overcoming faith in the human heart is Christ. When you are grafted deeply into him, you may win millions of lives to the faith. Jesus is the way, the truth, and the life, the secret to every hard problem in your heart. "Herein is our love made perfect, that we may have boldness in the day of judgment: because as he is, so are we in this world" (1 John 4:17). "Every man that hath this hope in him purifieth himself" (1 John 3:3).

And God confirms this faith in us, that we may be refined in the world, "not having spot, or wrinkle, or any such thing; but that we should be holy and without blemish" (Ephesians 5:27).

–40–

The Conviction of the Holy Spirit

God wants to set us on fire in the Holy Spirit so that we speak burning words. He wants to make all that we have so prophetic in all its bearings, that we will always speak as oracles of God. There ought to be something within us that shines through with a vital power—making others know we have seen God, and they feel God has come into their midst.

One day in a railroad carriage, I was drawing near to Cardiff, Wales, where I was scheduled to preach. So I washed my hands and face because I knew the moment I jumped off the train, I would have to rush out to the meeting. I had just a little season of prayer while washing. Meanwhile, the carriage had filled up with people who got on at Newport. When I returned, there were two ministerial gentlemen with the accustomed white collars. These two parsons cried out under conviction of sin, and in ten minutes the whole place was bathed in prayer and conviction.

We should be filled with the Holy Spirit to such an extent it would always be so. To be filled with the Holy Spirit and fire is a higher order, different from anything else.

-41-

Resisting Satan's Suggestions

John the Baptist is commonly called the forerunner of Jesus. Within his own short history, he had the power of God revealed to him as probably no other man in the old dispensation. He had a wonderful revelation. He had a mighty anointing. He moved Israel as the power of God rested upon him. God gave him a vision of Jesus, and he went forth with power and turned the hearts of Israel to God.

Have you noticed how satanic power can work in the mind? Look how Satan came to John when he was in prison. I find that Satan can come to any of us. Unless we are filled with the Spirit or divinely insulated with the power of God, we may fall by the power of Satan. But we have a greater power than Satan's—in imagination, in thought, in everything.

Satan came to John the Baptist in prison, and said, "Don't you think you have made a mistake? Here you are in prison. You hear nothing about Jesus. Isn't there something wrong with the whole business? After all, you may be greatly deceived about being a forerunner of the Christ."

I find men who might be giants of faith, who might be leaders of society, who might rise to subdue kingdoms, who might be noble among princes, but they go down because they allow the suggestions of Satan to dethrone their better knowledge of the power of God. God help us today! And he will.

−42−

The Unchanging Jesus

Now when John had heard in the prison the works of Christ, he sent two of his disciples, And said unto him, "Art thou he that should come, or do we look for another?" (Matthew 11:3).

How could Jesus send those men back to John the Baptist with a stimulating truth, with a personal, effective power that would convince them that they had met him whom all the prophets had spoken about? What would declare it? How shall they know? How can they tell it?

Jesus had an answer for John: "Go and show John again those things which ye do hear and see: The blind receive their sight, and the lame walk, the lepers are cleansed, and the deaf hear, the dead are raised up, and the poor have the gospel preached to them" (Matthew 11:4, 5).

When the two men saw the miracles and wonders and heard the gracious words he spoke as the power of God rested upon him, they were ready to tell John more about Jesus.

Has the work of Jesus come to an end? Instead of ending, it must continue. It is only by the grace of God that I dare make such a statement. Our Lord has not changed. He still performs miracles and wonders when we believe his Word. I have proved his Word countless times.

The big question is not whether he still performs miracles, but whether you will believe him for your need.

੨⊂➡ ੨⊂➡ ੨⊂➡

−43−

A Living Faith

To understand God's fullness, we must be filled with the Holy Spirit. God has a measure for us that cannot be measured by ordinary means. I am invited into this measure—the measure of the Lord Jesus Christ in me. But you cannot purify yourself; it is by the Blood of Jesus Christ, God's Son, that you are cleansed from all sin. When you are in relationship, sin is dethroned. When Jesus saw nothing but leaves on the tree in Mark 11:14, he said to this tree, "No man shall eat fruit of thee hereafter forever. And his disciples heard it."

The next morning, as they passed the same place, they saw the fig tree dried up from the roots. God's Son had spoken to the tree, and it could not live. He said to them, "Have faith in God" (Mark 11:22). We are his life. We are members of his body. The Spirit is in us, and there is no way to abide in the secret place of the Lord except by holiness and by being filled with the Word of God.

"The word of God is quick, and powerful, and sharper than any two edged sword, piercing even to the dividing asunder of soul and spirit and of the joints and marrow" (Hebrews 4:12).

One of the greatest things in the Word of God is that it discerns the thoughts and intents of the heart. Oh, that you may allow the Word of God to have perfect victory in your body so that it may be tingling through and through with God's divine power.

ॐ ॐ ॐ

-44-

The Christian Hope

Every believer belongs to the kingdom of heaven. Every believer has the life of the Lord in him. And if Jesus were to come, we would go out instantly to meet him because he is our life: "And your life is hid with Christ in God" (Colossians 3:3).

There is a wonderful word in Luke's Gospel, which brings great joy to our hearts: "And he said unto them, 'With desire I have desired to eat this Passover with you before I suffer. For I say unto you, I will not any more eat thereof, until it be fulfilled in the kingdom of God'" (Luke 22:15, 16).

I know there is a great deal of speculation on the rapture and on the coming of the Lord. But we are told to search the Scriptures, "For in them ye think ye have eternal life, and they are they which testify of me" (John 5:39). Here is the hope God has promised: "For the Lord himself shall descend from heaven with a shout, with the voice of the archangel, and with the trump of God; and the dead in Christ shall rise first. Then we which are alive and remain shall be caught up together with them in the clouds, to meet the Lord in the air: and so shall we ever be with the Lord. Wherefore comfort one another with these words" (1 Thessalonians 4:16, 17).

He could come today. Are you ready?

—45—

The Power in His Name

The kingdom of heaven is the life of Jesus; it is the power of the Highest. The kingdom of heaven is pure; it is holy. It has no disease, no imperfection. It is as holy as God is. And Satan with his evil power "cometh not, but for to steal, and to kill, and to destroy" that body (John 10:10).

I remember being invited to the home of a beautiful nine-year-old girl, who was possessed of an evil spirit. I took with me a much stronger and bigger man than myself. There we saw this child crying and rolling about from place to place. I got hold of the child to comfort her, but in a moment she twisted out of my hands like a serpent. How strange!

The big man who was with me said, "I'll take hold of the child." He took her, but the child, in a mysterious way, got out of his hands and went up some steps, crying bitterly and with a moaning that went right through us. The Spirit of the Lord came upon me; I went up the staircase, took hold of the child, looked right into her eyes, and said, "Come out, you evil spirit, in the Name of Jesus!" The child went to a couch close by and fell asleep, and from that day was perfect. Oh, this blessed Lord! Oh, this lovely Jesus! Oh, this incarnation of the Lamb slain!

ॐ ॐ ॐ

-46-

Under the Precious Blood

I know what Jesus meant when he said, "The kingdom of heaven is within you." He said that even the least in the kingdom of heaven is greater than John the Baptist. He meant all those who are under the Blood, those who have seen the Lord by faith, those who know that by redemption they are made sons of God. I say to you, he will never again taste the Passover until we are there with him. The kingdom will never be complete—it could not be—until we are all there at the great supper of the Lamb, where there will be millions and trillions of redeemed, which no man can number. We shall be there when that supper is taking place. I like to think of that.

I hope you will take one step into definite line with God and believe. It is an act of faith God wants to bring you into, a perfecting of love that cannot fail. It is a fact that he has opened the kingdom of heaven to all believers, and that he gives eternal life to them who believe. The Lord, the Omnipotent God, it is he who knoweth the end from the beginning, and has arranged by the Blood of the Lamb to cover the guilty and make intercession for all believers. Oh, it is a wonderful inheritance of faith to find shelter under the blood of Jesus!

> *Under the blood, the precious Blood,*
> *Under the cleansing, healing flood;*
> *Keep me, Saviour from day to day,*
> *Under the precious blood.*
> *- Eliza Edmunds Hewitt*

Trusting the One Who Knows All About You

If you are whole from top to bottom and don't know you have a body, it is easy to shout, "Glory!" But if some people shouted, "Glory," one side of them would ache. And so it is with people who are not free. I want to free you and put you in a place where you can and will shout, "Glory!"

It is true that God keeps me, as it were, without knowing I have a body. I believe that is "redemption." But I am not going to condemn people who have not yet arrived at this wonderful place in their spiritual walk. God sends me around the world to help people who are in need. But I cannot help them unless I give them the Word of God. If I can lay down a basis in the Word, I can send them home and know God will deliver them.

When Satan can get to your body, he will make the pain or the weakness so distracting, that it will affect your mind and bring your mind down to the level of the pain. When that takes place, you haven't the same freedom in the Spirit to lift up your heart and to shout and praise the Lord.

Does God know your weaknesses? Is he thoroughly acquainted with you? Yes, he knows more about you than you do.

Why not trust him who knows all about you instead of telling somebody else who knows only what you have told them?

-48-

Claiming Our God-given Rights

A nything that takes me away from God's presence is evil and of Satan. This includes things that rob me of my worship, my peace, my joy, and my consciousness of God's presence. God enables me to lift myself up and live in the world as though I was not of it (because I *am not* of it). By the Word of God, we know that the kingdom of heaven is within us. "Greater is he that is in you"—which is the kingdom of heaven, which is the Son of God—"than he that is in the world"—the power of Satan outside you (1 John 4:4).

In one service, I called for anyone suffering with pain in the back, legs, head, or shoulders to stand. A young man stood who was suffering in his leg. I asked him to stand in the aisle as an example for all the people.

First, I asked him if he was saved. He was. Then I asked him if he believed the kingdom of God was within him. "I do," he answered.

To prove that the presence of God and the Scriptures were within him and against the power of Satan, I told him to say, "In the name of Jesus, come out!" I told him to shout and put his hand on his leg and say, "In the name of Jesus, I command you to come out!" Then I told him to walk around, and asked if Satan had come out, and whether he was free.

"Yes," he said. Praise God!

How much more would be done if we would inwardly claim our God-given rights!

૨¢► ૨¢► ૨¢►

–49–

In Remembrance of Me

When Jesus called his disciples together for the last supper before he went to the cross, he instructed them "Do this in remembrance of me" (Luke 22:19). He took the cup, he took the bread, and he gave thanks.

The very attitude of giving thanks for his shed blood and for his broken body overwhelms the heart. To think that my Lord could give thanks for his own shed blood! To think that my Lord could give thanks for his broken body! Only divinity can reveal this sublime act to our hearts! The natural man cannot receive it, but the spiritual man, the man who has been created anew by faith in Christ, is open to it. The person who believes God is inborn with the eternal seed of truth, righteousness, and faith. And from the moment he sees truth, he is made a new creation. Then, the flesh ceases, the spiritual man begins. One passes off, the other passes on. I say the Lord brings a child of faith into a place of rest, causes him to sit with him in heavenly places, gives him a language in the Spirit, and makes him know he no longer belongs to the law of creation.

Jesus said, "Take, eat; this is my body." We can have a real knowledge of Christ through this emblem, when we take from the table of the riches of his promises. The riches of Heaven are before us. Fear not, only believe, for God has opened the treasures of his holy Word.

–50–

The Gift of Tongues

People ask, "Do all speak with tongues?" Certainly not. But all people **may** speak as the Spirit gives utterance just as they did in the upper room (Acts 2), and as they did in the house of Cornelius (Acts 10), and as happened at Ephesus (Acts 19) when they were filled with the Holy Ghost.

There is quite a difference between having a gift and speaking as the Spirit gives utterance. If I had been given a gift when I was filled with the Holy Ghost, I could have spoken, because gifts and calling remain. But I couldn't speak in tongues. Why? Because I had received the Holy Ghost, but I hadn't received the gift of tongues.

I had, however, received the Holy Ghost, who is the giver of all gifts. Nine months after receiving the Holy Spirit, God gave me the gift of tongues so that I could speak in tongues at any time. But do I? God forbid! Why? Because no man ought to use a gift. It is the Holy Ghost who uses the gift.

Tongues with Interpretation: "The Spirit of the Lord breathes upon the slain, and upon the dry bones, and upon the things which are not, and changes them in the flesh in a moment of time, and makes that which is weak, strong. And behold, he is among us tonight to quicken that which is dead and make the dead alive."

–51–

Spiritual Warfare

People often come to me and say, "I have been prayed for, and I am just the same."

It is enough to make you kick them! No, I would not kick them. I am the last man to kick anybody. God forbid! "For the weapons of our warfare are not carnal, but mighty through God to the pulling down of strongholds" (1 Corinthians 10:4).

If I can get you enraged against the powers of darkness and the powers of disease, if I can awaken you, you won't go to bed without proving that there is a Master in you who is greater than the power that is hanging 'round about you. So many times I have gone into houses where I've been shut up with insane people. I have gone in, determined that they should be delivered. Often, in the middle of the night, but sometimes in the middle of the day, demon powers would come and bite me, and handle me terribly roughly. I never gave in to them. It would dethrone a higher principle if I had to give in.

There is a great cloud of witnesses of the satanic powers from hell. We are here on probation to slay the enemy, destroy the kingdoms of darkness, to move among satanic forces, and to subdue them in the name of Jesus. May the God of grace and mercy strengthen us.

-52-

Our Greatest Inheritance

The great plan of God's salvation is redemption in its fullness. Understanding the fourth chapter of Romans will greatly increase our faith. It is a very marvelous word, and God wants us to fully comprehend the fullness of what it means. There are things in this chapter that will bring a revelation of what God means for the man who believes.

While I know prayer is wonderful, and that it not only changes **things** but changes **you**; while I know the man of prayer can go right in and take the blessing from God; yet I tell you that if we grasp the truth that we have before us, we shall find that faith is the greatest inheritance of all.

May God give us faith that will bring this glorious inheritance into our hearts. It is true that the just shall live by faith, but do not forget that it takes a just person to live by faith.

May the Lord reveal to us the fullness of this truth that God gave to Abraham. When Abraham trusted God for a son, he dared not look at either Sarah or himself. He had to look at God. That is where you need to look in your hour of need, and you can depend on him: he will not fail!

> *Lord, I believe, Lord, I believe!*
> *Savior, raise my faith in thee,*
> *Till it can move a mountain.*
> *- Anonymous*

⧓ ⧓ ⧓

-53-

He Is Just the Same Today

One day a man by the name of Jairus fell at Jesus' feet. He and his wife were in serious trouble. Their little daughter was lying at the point of death. Everything they had tried had failed, but they knew that if they found Jesus, she would be made whole.

When Jairus found Jesus, he besought him greatly, saying, "My little daughter lieth at the point of death: I pray thee, come and lay thy hands on her that she may be healed; and she shall live." And Jesus went with him (Mark 5:22-24).

I want you to know that this same Jesus is with you today. He is right here with his ministry of power and blessing. For we note that as Jesus went with the man, something happened.

"While he yet spake, there came from the ruler of the synagogue's house certain which said, 'Thy daughter is dead. Why troublest thou the Master any further?'" (Mark 5:35). But Jesus encouraged the ruler of the synagogue and said, "Be not afraid, only believe" (verse 36). Ah, what things God does for us when we only believe. He is rich to all who call upon him. What possibilities there are in our lives if we would only believe in that divine presence, for God is with us in the power of his Spirit.

Do you dare rise and claim your healing? Do you dare rise and claim your rights of perfect health? All things are possible to him that believeth.

Only believe! Only believe!
All things are possible, only believe!

≈ ≈ ≈

-54-

Christ Jesus, Our Only Place of Safety

A man possessed with demon power and sickness and every weakness came to Jesus. Jesus cast the evil spirits out, and the man was made whole. But instead of seeking the Holy Spirit and the light of God—like blind Bartimaeus did after he was healed—his man went to the first worldly entertainment he saw (Matthew 12:43-45; Luke 11:24-26). God save us!

Healing power is for the glory of God, and it appears that this man was swept and garnished. The evil spirit had nowhere to go, so it returned and found the man had no inhabitant within him. Christ and the power of the Spirit were not there, and so the evil spirit entered into the man and his case was worse than before.

If you want healing by the power of God, it means your life has to be filled with God. Will it last? Get Jesus on board, and it lasts forever.

What are you going to do with this truth? None is safe without Christ. Are you willing to so surrender yourself to God today so that Satan shall have no dominion over you? In the name of Jesus, I ask you to do so.

> *The power of God is just the same today.*
> *It doesn't matter what the people say,*
> *Whatever God has promised, he is able to perform,*
> *For the power of God is just the same today.*
> *- Author Unknown*

-55-

Following God's Leading

When you believe God, he sets his seal upon you. The evil one dare not break it. He dare not break into your life because he has no power there.

There is a righteousness, which is made known only to the person who knows God, and there are certain things that God can reveal only to the man who believes him.

One of the greatest scriptural passages that illustrates God's plan is when he worked in Abraham, which was exactly opposite to human nature. Abraham's wife Sarah had many good points, but she had not reached the place of believing God. She laughed when God told Abraham that they would have a son. Then she denied having done so. When they waited a time, and she saw that their bodies were growing more frail, she said, "Now it will be just as good for you to take Hagar for a wife and bring forth a son through her" (Genesis 16:2).

But that was not the seed of Abraham of which God spoke. Their actions caused a great deal of trouble in the house of Abraham. There are times when you dare not take another's advice. The person who walks with God can only afford to follow God's leadings. His leadings are direct and clear, and the evidence is so real that every day you know that God is with you, unfolding his plan to you. That is what I like about being in the will of God.

-56-

Born of God

Thank God, there is a higher order than that under which natural man operates. And he wants to bring us into this higher order where we will believe him. Think of the life of Abraham, who believed God for a son.

In the first place, God promised Abraham a son. Could a child be born into the world, except in accordance with natural law? It was when all natural law was finished, and when there was no substance in Abraham and Sarah, that the law of the Spirit brought forth a son. It was the law of faith in God who had promised. We are born not only of blood and by the will of the flesh, but also of God (John 3:3).

Sometimes I see that this power within us is greater when we are weak than when we are strong, just as this power was greater in Abraham in his latter years than when he was strong physically.

Listen to what the apostle Paul wrote: "He [the Lord] said unto me, My grace is sufficient for thee: for my strength is made perfect in weakness. Most gladly therefore will I rather glory in my infirmities, that the power of Christ may rest upon me. Therefore I take pleasure in infirmities, in reproaches, in distresses for Christ's sake: for when I am weak, then am I strong" (2 Corinthians 12:9, 10).

૱ ૱ ૱

-57-

Superseding the Natural Law

One of the best illustrations of someone believing God for the impossible—on natural lines—is when God gave a son to Abraham and Sarah when they were long past their child-bearing years.

Sarah had a difficult time believing it would ever happen. But Abraham refused to look at his own either body or Sarah's; he believed that the promise would come to pass. Perhaps you are in need of a healing, and you know that according to the natural life, there is no virtue in your body to give you that health. Maybe the ailment from which you suffer has so drained your life and energy, that there is no help at all in you.

But God says that you shall be healed if you believe. It makes no difference how your body is. It was exactly the helplessness of Sarah and of Abraham that brought the glorious fact that a son was born.

God wants you to know today that there is no limitation with him, and he wants to bring us to a place where there will be no limitation in us. This will happen by the working of the Omnipotent in us continually—greater than any science or any power in the world—and bringing us into the place to comprehend God and man.

-58-

Faith Brings Grace

I am saved by the power of God because of the promise that God made to Abraham (see Romans 4), that his children would be as the countless sands upon the seashore and as the stars in multitude and glory. Everyone who comes to Christ and is saved is part of spiritual Abraham.

I want you to see that Romans 4:16 has the answer for help beyond the natural: "Therefore it is of faith, that it might be by grace; to the end the promise might be sure to all the seed; not to that only which is of the law, but to that also which is of the faith of Abraham; who is the father of us all."

Do you need a touch in your body? Do you need a touch in your spirit? Do you desire to be baptized in the Holy Ghost and filled with all of God's power? Here is the answer for you: "That the blessing of Abraham might come on the Gentiles through Jesus Christ; that we might receive the promise of the Spirit through faith" (Galatians 3:14).

Despite Sarah's unbelief concerning God's promise that she would bear a son in her old age (see Genesis 18), Abraham knew God had spoken and would keep his word.

If God has spoken to you about some impossible situation (in the natural, that is), do not laugh as Sarah did. Begin to believe and do not give up. The answer comes by faith: "Therefore it is of faith, that it might be by grace."

–59–

Accomplishing the Impossible

The story of Abraham and Sarah inspires me to believe God for the impossible in the natural. Their bodies are dead as far as creating a child. It is impossible for Sarah to conceive.

But God tells Abraham, "As it is written, I have made thee a father of many nations" (Romans 4:17). "Now, then," Abraham reasons, "God has made me a father of many nations, and there is no hope of a son according to the natural law—no hope whatever." During the previous twenty years of waiting, the conditions had grown more and more hopeless. But the promise had been made.

Now, my friend, how long have you been with your rheumatism or other afflictions and needs? How long have you been waiting for the promise and it has not come? Had you need to wait? Look here! I want to tell you that all the people who are saved are blessed with faithful Abraham. Abraham is the great substance of the whole keynote of Scripture; a man who dared for twenty-five years to believe God when everything worsened with each passing day.

Oh, beloved, there is not a subject in the whole Bible that makes my body aflame with passions after God and his righteousness as this does. I see that he never fails. He wants us to believe, and then we shall never fail.

–60–

God Will Make It Right

Whenever I read that God made Abraham "the father of many nations" (Genesis 17:5; Romans 4:17), I feel like weeping, for it was impossible for Abraham and Sarah to have a child to fulfill God's declaration that Abraham would be the father of many nations. But then he gave them Isaac! My cup runneth over as I see the magnitude of this living God.

You talk about your infirmities—look at this! I have never felt I have had an infirmity since I understood this chapter (Romans 4). O God, help me—"As it is written, I have made thee a father of many nations, before him whom he believed, even God, who quickeneth the dead, and calleth those things which be not as though they were" (Romans 4:17).

I will not look at my body, I will not look at my infirmities—I believe God will make the whole thing right. What does it matter if I have not heard for over twenty years? God is reality and wants us to know that if we will believe, it shall be perfect. Read that passage again: "Who quickeneth the dead, and calleth those things that be not as though they were."

Count on it, friend, there is no limitation of possibilities when our faith is anchored in God.

-61-

Help During Testing Time

The Scripture tells us that the delaying of the promise and the testing of Abraham was the seed of future generations who believed in God. "And being fully persuaded that, what he had promised, he was able also to perform" (Romans 4:21). Therefore, it was imputed unto him for righteousness, and not to him only, but to you and everyone else who believes.

Have you ever been tested? It is the greatest thing in the world to be tested. You never know what you are made of until you are tested. Some people say, "Oh, I don't know why my lot is such a heavy one," and God puts them into the fire again. He knows how to do it, I can tell you—he is a blessed God. There is no such thing as a groan when God gets hold of you. When we really get in the will of God, he can make our enemies to be at peace with us. It is wonderful.

Listen to these words and take them into your being, for they will keep you during testing times: "There hath no temptation taken you but such as is common to man; but God is faithful, who will not suffer you to be tempted above that ye are able, but will with the temptation also make a way to escape, that ye may be able to bear it" (1 Corinthians 10:13).

-62-

Dare You Trust Him?

I wonder if you really believe that God can quicken that which is dead. I have seen it any number of times. Despite the fact that in the natural there was no hope for Sarah to give birth to a child, Abraham believed in hope.

Sometimes Satan can so blur your mind and interfere with your perception that he brings that obscure condition right between you and God. But God is able to change the whole position if you will let him have a chance. Turn your back on every sense of unbelief, and believe God. Do you want to feel the touch of God? God will bring it to you.

Abraham had a good time in his relationship with God. The more he was squeezed, the more he rejoiced. And being not weak in faith, he considered not his own body, which was now dead when he was about one hundred years old. Neither did he consider the deadness of Sarah's womb. "He staggered not at the promise of God through unbelief; but was strong in faith, giving glory to God" (Romans 4:20).

Now look at Abraham's faith as given in the next verse: "And being fully persuaded that what he had promised, he was able to perform" (Romans 4:21).

"He staggered not … through unbelief." God knows. He has a plan. He has a way. Dare you trust him?

-63-

Submission to the King

Is it possible to have controversy and strife in the same household? Certainly. A good example is in Abraham and Sarah's house after Isaac was born. You can read about it in Genesis 21. The story begins when Sarah saw Ishmael—Abraham's son through Hagar—teasing Isaac. Here we see strife between Ishmael, the seed of the flesh, and Isaac, the seed of promise. Eventually, Abraham cast out Hagar and Ishmael with God's approval.

Dear friend, there is nothing that is going to hold you except the Isaac life—the seed of Abraham. You will find that the flesh life will always have to be cast out. It was very hard to do, but it had to be done.

You say, "How hard!" Yes, but how long had it to be? Till submission came; and I tell you that there will always be jealousy and strife in your hearts and lives till flesh is destroyed—till Isaac controls and rules in authority over the whole body. And when the Isaac power reigns over you, you will find that the whole of your life is full of peace and joy.

God is a reality. God is true, and in him there is no lie, neither shadow of turning.

-64-

Keeping God's Secrets

A time came in Abraham's life that God tested him to the limit. That is when God told this man of faith to sacrifice Isaac, his son of promise. "Take now thy son, thine only son Isaac," he told Abraham, "and offer him there for a burnt-offering upon one of the mountains which I will tell thee of" (Genesis 22:2).

Do you think Abraham told anybody of this command? No, I am sure he did not, because Isaac was so near to his heart. Abraham believed that just as miraculously as Isaac came into the world, God could even miraculously raise him though he were slain. When God tells you a secret, do not tell anyone else. God will, perchance, tell you to go and lay hands on some sick one. Go, do it, and do not tell anyone.

God can captivate my thoughts in such a way that they may be entirely for him. When God is in control of your heart, you will see that every thought is captive, that everything is brought into obedience, and is brought into a place where you are in dominion because Christ is enthroned in your life (2 Corinthians 1:4, 5).

God reveals deep and special things to certain people. Keep your counsel with God.

꽃 꽃 꽃

-65-

God's Help During Temptations

God told Abraham that he must offer Isaac on the altar. What a strange turn of events. Isaac—the heart of his heart, the promised son—whom God said was to be the seed of all living.

You might think that you are tried more than other people are. If you knew the value of it, you would praise God for trial more than for anything. It is the trial that purifies you; it is through the fiery furnace of affliction that God gets you in the place where he can use you.

The person who has no trials and no difficulties is the person whom God dare not allow Satan to touch because he could not stand temptation. But Jesus will not allow any person to be tempted more than he is able to bear (1 Corinthians 10:13). The Scriptures are the strongest evidence of anything you can have. Before Abraham offered Isaac, he was tried, and God knew he could do it; and, before God puts you through the furnace of afflictions, he knows you will go through, and not one single temptation comes to any person more than he is able to bear; and with the temptation, God is always there to help you through.

That was exactly the position in the case of Abraham. He was tempted, but God helped him through to victory.

꒞ ꒞ ꒞

−66−

An Inheritance of the Spirit

If you are convinced that you need the baptism of the Holy Spirit, and you know it is in the Scriptures, never rest till God gives it to you. If you know it is scriptural for you to be healed of every weakness, never rest till God makes it yours. If you know that the Scriptures teach holiness, purity, and divine likeness—overcoming under all conditions—never rest till you are an overcomer. If you know that God has given visions to his people, making the Scriptures come alive, never rest till you have the same experience.

You ask, "Have you a Scripture to prove it?" Yes, the Scripture says that you "may be able to comprehend with all saints what is the breadth, and length, and depth, and height; and to know the love of God" (Ephesians 3:18, 19).

Unknown Tongues with Interpretation: "Oh, hallelujah! This blessed inheritance of the Spirit is come to profit withal—teaching you all things, and making you understand that the will of God cometh not by observation, but holy men of old spoke and wrote as the Spirit gave them power and utterance, and so today the Holy Ghost must fill us with this same initiative of God."

⟨⟐ ⟨⟐ ⟨⟐

-67-

A Pattern for Righteousness

We must live in the fire; we must hate sin; we must love righteousness; we must live with God, for he says we must be blameless and harmless amidst the crooked positions of the world. Beloved, God is able to confirm all you have heard and read about going through testings, which are the greatest blessings you can have.

God wants to make us like Jesus. Think about the loftiness of the character of Jesus, who was a firstfruit to make us pure and holy. I see Jesus going about clothed with power. And I see you, a child of God, clothed with power. Jesus was a firstfruit, the pattern of God.

In Jesus, God has not given us a pattern that is impossible to copy. Beloved, Jesus hated sin. If I have hatred for sin, I have something that is worth millions. Oh, the Blood of Jesus Christ, God's Son, cleanseth us from all sin.

Beloved, I believe that the hope of the Church for the future is in its being purified—made like unto Jesus, pure in heart, pure in thought. Then, when a believer lays hands upon the sick, Satan has no power; when he commands him to leave, Satan has to go.

What a redemption! What a baptism! What an unction! It is ecstasy of delight beyond expression for the soul to live and move in him who is our being.

❧ ❧ ❧

-68-

God Offers a Better Way

As we look back over our spiritual journey, we can see that there has been a good deal of our own way, and that the end of our way was the beginning of God's way. We cannot enter into the deep things of God until we are free from our own ideas and ways.

When we think of Jacob, we think of the supplanter (or one who takes by trickery). But when Jacob came to the end of his way, God had his way for the supplanter. How slow we are to see that God has a better way for each one of us. Beloved, the glory is never so wonderful as when God has his way, when we are helpless, and throw down our sword, and give up our authority to him.

Jacob was a great worker and he would go through any hardship if he could only have his way. In many things, he had his way, and how mercifully God preserved him from calamity.

There is a way that seems good, but the end of that way is death, but God has his very best for each of his own, a higher standard for us than we have yet attained.

It is the goodness of the Lord that leads to repentance, and I believe that if ever Jacob was conscious of his own meanness, it was when God revealed his wonderful goodness to him.

Many things may happen in our lives to show us how depraved we are by nature, but when the veil is lifted, we see how merciful and tender God is. His tender compassion is over us all the time. Oh, how wonderful it is to be where God is!

ॐ ॐ ॐ

-69-

Faithfulness

And Jacob was left alone; and there wrestled a man with him until the breaking of the day (Genesis 32:24).

Jacob and his mother devised an evil plan to obtain the family blessing from Isaac. But how inglorious was the fulfilling of this carnal plan: "Esau hated Jacob because of the blessing wherewith his father blessed him: and Esau said in his heart, "The days of mourning for my father are at hand; then will I slay my brother Jacob" (Genesis 27:41).

Our own plans lead us so frequently into disaster. Jacob had to flee from the land, but how gracious the Lord was to that fleeing fugitive. God planned a ladder and the angels that Jacob would see (Genesis 28:12). Our God is so gracious that he refused to have his plans of grace frustrated by the carnal workings of Jacob's mind. So he revealed himself to Jacob, saying, "I am with thee, and will keep thee in all places whither thou goest, and will bring thee again into this land; for I will not leave thee, until I have done that which I have spoken to thee of (Genesis 28:15).

Since the time that Jacob saw the revelation of the ladder and the angels (Genesis 28), he had twenty-one years of wandering, fighting, and struggling. But God was faithful to his promise all those years.

୧◑ ୧◑ ୧◑

Alone with God

As Jacob returned to the land of his birth, his heart was full of fear. If ever he needed the Lord, it was just at this time. He had tricked his brother Esau years earlier, had never made it right, and he knew his brother had vowed to kill him. Jacob wanted to be alone with God.

Oh, to be left alone! Alone with God!

In the context of Genesis 32, we read that all that he owned had crossed over the brook Jabok. His wives had gone over; his children had gone over; his sheep and oxen had gone over; his camels and asses had gone over; all had gone over. He was alone. The Lord saw Jacob's need and came down and met with him. It was the Lord, himself, who wrestled with the supplanter (Genesis 32:24), breaking him, changing him, transforming him. Jacob was brought to a place of absolute weakness. He knew that his brother Esau had power to take away all that he owned and execute vengeance upon him. He knew that there was only one kind of deliverance. No one could deliver him but God. And there alone, lean in soul and impoverished in spirit, he met with God.

Oh, we need to get alone with God; we need to be broken; we need to be changed; we need to be transformed. And when we meet with God, when he interposes, all care and strife is at an end. Get alone with God and receive the revelation of his infinite grace and of his wonderful purposes and plans for your life.

-71-

Repentance Brings Forgiveness and Power

Jacob is a good example of a person who had to get rid of a lot of things when he met God at Peniel (Genesis 32:24-30). It had been all Jacob! Jacob! Jacob!

Hour after hour passed. Oh, that we might spend all night alone with God! We are occupied too much with the things of time and sense. We need the presence of God. We need to give God time if we are to receive new revelations from him. We need to get past all the thoughts of earthly matters that crowd in so rapidly. We need to give God time to deal with us. It is only after he has dealt with us, as he dealt with Jacob, that we can have power with him and prevail.

Jacob was not dry-eyed that night. Hosea tells us, "He wept and made supplication" (Hosea 12:4). He knew he had been a disappointment to the Lord; he had been a groveler. But in the revelation he received as he wrestled that night, he saw the possibility of being transformed from a supplanter to a prince with God. The testing hour came when, at break of day, the angel, who was none other than the Lord of Hosts, said to him, "Let me go, for the day breaketh" (Genesis 32:26). Jacob knew that if God left without blessing him, he could not meet Esau. Likewise, you cannot meet the terrible things that await you in the world unless you receive the blessing of God. Seek him today!

Power with God

You must never let go whatever you are seeking—fresh revelation, light on the path, some particular need—never let go. Victory is ours if we are earnest enough. If darkness covers you, if it is a fresh revelation you need, or your mind needs relief, or there are problems that you know you cannot solve, lay hold of God and declare, "I will not let thee go, except thou bless me" (Genesis 32:26).

That is what Jacob cried. And God blessed him and declared, "Thy name shall be called no more Jacob, but Israel; for as a prince hast thou power with God and with men, and hast prevailed" (Genesis 32:28). Now a new order was beginning. The old supplanter passed away. There was a new creation, and Jacob, the supplanter, was transformed into Israel, the prince.

When God comes into your life, you will find him enough for all time and all eternity. As Israel comes forth, the sun rises upon him, and he has power over all the things of the world, and power over Esau.

When he met Esau, there was no fighting, but a blessed reconciliation. They kissed each other. "When a man's ways please the Lord, he maketh even his enemies to be at peace with him" (Proverbs 16:7).

What a wonderful change! The material things do not count for much after a night of revelation from our God.

-73-

He Will Never Leave You

Can you hold God? Yes, you can. Sincerity can hold him; dependence can hold him; weakness can hold him. It is when you are weak that then you are strong (2 Corinthians 12:10). But I will tell you what cannot hold him. Self-righteousness cannot hold him; money cannot hold him; presumption cannot hold him; high-mindedness cannot hold him (thinking you are something when you are nothing, puffed up in your own imagination). But sincerity can hold him. You can hold him in the prayer closet, in the prayer meeting, everywhere. If you become lukewarm, instead of being at white heat, you become a disappointment to God.

There may be a thought sometimes that God has left you. Oh, no. He had promised not to leave Jacob, and he did not fail in his promise (Genesis 28:15). He has promised not to leave us, and he will not fail. We need to get alone with God, to have a real meeting with God. He will bring us down. He will change our names. He will transform us from Jacob to Israel. But we need to lay hold of him.

If God does not help me, I am no good for this world's need. I am no longer salt. It is so easy to lose the savor. But as we get alone with God and meet with him and he gives us his blessing, he re-salts us; he empowers us; he brings us to brokenness, and moves us into the orbit of his own perfect will.

Dependence Upon God

And Jacob called the name of the place Peniel: for I have seen God face to face, and my life is preserved. And as he passed over Peniel the sun rose upon him, and he halted upon his thigh (Genesis 32:30, 31).

You might ask, "What is the use of a lame man?" It is those who have seen the face of God and have been broken by him that can meet the forces of the enemy and break down the bulwarks of Satan's kingdom. It is the lame that take the prey (Isaiah 33:23). Jacob was brought to a place of dependence upon God.

It is when we have the revelation of Calvary, and see that we ourselves are good for nothing, and that God counts us as good for nothing, and has crucified our old natures upon that rugged cross, and has made the cross of Christ real in our lives so that we are broken, that we can come forth to a life of dependence upon the power of the Holy Spirit. Henceforth, we are nothing without him; we are absolutely dependent upon him. I am absolutely nothing without the power and unction of the Holy Ghost. Oh, for a life of absolute dependence! It is only a life of dependence that is a life of power. If you are not there, get alone with God, let him change and transform you, and never let him go until he blesses you and makes you an Israel, a prince with God.

-75-

God Prevailing Through Us

For our Scripture today, let us turn to Acts 19:1-20. This wonderful reading has many things in it that indicate to us that there was something in the baptism in the Holy Spirit more marvelous than human power. When I think about Pentecost, I am astonished from day to day because of its mightiness, of its wonderfulness, and how glory overshadows it. I think sometimes about these things, and they make me feel we have barely touched the glory. Truly, it is so, but we must thank God that we **have** touched it. Whatever God has done in the past, his name is still the same. When hearts are burdened, and they come face to face with the need of the day, they look into God's Word and it brings in a propeller of power, an anointing that makes you know he has truly visited.

There are many waters to cross and all kinds of difficult times until we get to the real summit of everything. The power of God is with us to prevail. God is with us. When God has you in his own plan, what a change! Then things operate differently. You see things in a new light. God is being glorified as you yield from day to day, and the Spirit seems to lay hold of you and lead you on. Yes, God's Spirit is pressing on, and then he gives us touches of his wonderful power, manifestations of the glory of these things and indications of greater things to follow, and these days in which we are living speak of better days. How wonderful!

-76-

Victory Over Every Difficulty

There is a very blessed place for you to attain. The place where God wants you is a place of victory. When the Spirit of the Lord comes into your life, it must be victory. The disciples, before they received the Holy Ghost, were always in bondage.

But beloved, after they received the power of the Holy Spirit, they were made like lions to meet any difficulty. They were made to stand any test. When the power of God fell upon them in the upper room, they came out in front of all those people who were gathered together and accused them of crucifying the Lord of glory. They were bold.

What had made them so? I will tell you. Purity is bold. Take, for instance, a little child. They will gaze straight into your eyes for as long as you like, without winking once. The more pure, the more bold; and I tell you God wants to bring us into that divine purity of heart and life—that holy boldness. Not officiousness; not swelled-headedness; not self-righteousness; but a pure, holy, divine appointment by one who will come in and live with you, defying the powers of Satan, and standing you in a place of victory—overcoming the world.

You will never inherit this from the flesh. This is a gift of God by the Spirit to all who obey. It is the personality of the Deity. It is God in you.

☙ ☙ ☙

Being Bold for God

Do you think that God would make you be a failure? God never made man to be a failure. He made man to be a "son," to walk about the earth in power. When I look at you, I see your potential to control and bring everything into subjection. Yes, there is the capacity of the power of Christ to dwell in you, to bring every evil thing under you till you can put your feet upon it, and be master over the flesh and the devil. Then nothing within you rises, except that which will magnify and glorify the Lord.

God wants me to remind you of the disciples, who were so frail, like you and me. And like them, we, too, may now be filled with God and become pioneers of this wonderful truth I preach.

We see Peter, frail, helpless, and at every turn of the tide, a failure. And God filled him with the Spirit of his righteousness till he went up and down, bold as a lion. And when he came to death—even crucifixion—he counted himself unworthy of being crucified like his Lord. He asked that his murderers put him head downwards on the tree. Here we see a changed man. We see Peter with a deep submissiveness and a power that was greater than all flesh.

That is what the power of God can do for you!

-78-

Becoming a New Person

The Scriptures do not tell two stories. They tell the truth. I want you to know the truth, and the truth will set you free. What is truth? Jesus said, "I am the way, the truth, and the life" (John 14:6). "He that believeth on me, as the Scripture hath said, out of his belly shall flow rivers of living water" (John 7:38). This he spake of the Spirit that should be given them after he was glorified.

I do not find anything in the Bible but holiness, and nothing in the world but worldliness. Therefore, if I live in the world, I shall become worldly; but, on the other hand, if I live in the Bible, I shall become holy. This is the truth, and the truth will set you free.

The power of God can remodel you. He can make you hate sin and love righteousness. He can take away bitterness and hatred and covetousness and malice, and can so consecrate you by his power, through his blood, that you are made pure—every bit holy. Pure in mind, heart, and actions—pure right through. God has given me the way of life, and I want to give it to you, as though this were the last day I had to live.

Jesus is the best there is for you, and you can have him today if you do not know him as your Savior and Lord. God gave his Son for your sins, and for the sins of the whole world.

Walking in the Newness of Life

Jesus came to make us free from sin, disease, and pain. When I see any who are diseased and in pain, I have great compassion for them. I know God intends people to be so filled with him that the power of sin shall have no effect upon them, and they shall go forth, as I am doing, to help the needy, sick, and afflicted.

But what is the main thing? To preach the kingdom of God and his righteousness. Jesus came to do this. John came preaching repentance. The disciples began by preaching repentance towards God, and faith in the Lord Jesus Christ.

Through the revelation of the Word of God, we find that divine healing is solely for the glory of God, and salvation is to make you know that now you are inhabited by another, even God, and you are to walk with God in newness of life.

I tell you, God is able to so transform, change, and bring you into order by the Spirit, that you become a new creation after God's order. There is no such thing as defeat for the believer. Without the cross, without Christ's righteousness, without the new birth, without the indwelling Christ, without this divine incoming of God, I am a failure. But God, the Holy Ghost, comes in and takes our place till we are renewed in righteousness—made the sons of God.

–*80*–

Christ, the Son of the Living God

Jesus asked his disciples one of the most important questions in the Bible in Matthew 16:13: "Whom do men say that I the Son of man am?" In verse 16, we read Simon Peter's answer: "Thou art the Christ, the Son of the living God."

There is a tremendous divine treasure within the human soul that comes into line with this truth. This truth gives us the authority and power to not only bind and loose, but also to be able by the grace of God to stand so that the gates of hell shall not be able to prevail against us.

Beloved, what I am desiring above all is that I shall be emblematic of this truth in every way; that this word shall be in me a light, a flame of fire burning in my bones.

Never forget that we are born of God (John 1:12, 13). Having his nature. Born of God. This divine nature we have received came to us when we received the Word of God. When he said to them, whom do ye say that I am? Peter answered, "Thou art the Christ." Wonderful! Wonderful!

I am making it personal today. Whom do you say that he is, today? Oh, glory to God! Whom do you say he is? The Christ! The Son of the living God! And the truth comes to us: "Blessed are thou ... for flesh and blood hath not revealed it unto thee, but my Father which is in heaven" (Matthew 16:17).

He is the Son of God, and he was manifested to destroy the works of the devil.

–81–

Reigning with Christ

The words of Jesus to his disciples have a special meaning for us regarding our position as believers: "Nevertheless I tell you the truth; It is expedient for you that I go away: for if I go not away, the Comforter will not come unto you; but if I depart, I will send him unto you. And when he is come, he will reprove the world of sin, and of righteousness, and of judgment. Of sin, because they believe not on me; of righteousness, because I go to my Father, and ye see me no more; of judgment, because the prince of this world is judged" (John 16:7-11).

Sin. Righteousness. Judgment. These are divine relationships after we have received the Holy Ghost.

> *Sin*—because they believe not on me.
> *Righteousness*—because I go unto the Father.
> *Judgment*—because the prince of this world is judged.

Oh, that we may be aroused to our privileges, to see that we reign with Christ in this place over the powers of the world. God wants to bring us into the knowledge of this truth. We are truly in the place where "greater is he that is within you than he that is in the world." We are truly in the apostolic position, and have the right to take our place on the authority of God in this world.

-82-

A Rock and a Key

The new birth gives us a royal status. We can reign over the powers of darkness, bringing everything into perfect submission to the rightful owner, and that is the Lord. He it is that rules and reigns within. Our bodies have become temples of the Holy Ghost.

He said to Peter: "Upon this rock will I build my church" (Matthew 16:18). What rock was it? The rock is the living Word. Upon this rock will I build my church. What is the rock? The Son of the living God.

Then Jesus said he would give them the keys to the kingdom of heaven (verse 19). He is the rock, but what are the keys? The keys are the divine working by faith the things of God. Jesus goes on to say that he would give them the keys for unlocking the kingdom of heaven. Remember this. It is the key, which has life within it. It is the key, which has the power to enter in. It is life divine. That verse 19 opens and unlocks all the dark things, and brings life and liberty to the captive. "Upon this rock I will build my church; and the gates of hell shall not prevail against it."

ॐ ॐ ॐ

Power to Run the Race

The necessity that seven men be chosen for the position of "serving tables" was very evident in the early church (Acts 6). In verse five, we read: "And the saying pleased the whole multitude, and they chose Stephen, a man full of faith and of the Holy Ghost, and Philip." There were others, of course, but Stephen and Philip stand out most prominently in the Scriptures. Philip was a man so filled with the Holy Spirit that wherever he went, a revival always followed. Stephen was a man so filled with divine power, that although serving tables might have been all right in the minds of the other disciples, God had a greater vision for him—a baptism of fire, of power, and of divine unction. His experience took him to the climax of his life, when he saw right into the open heavens.

When we please God in our daily ministration, we find that everyone who is faithful in little measure, God will use in a greater measure. We have such an example in Stephen—a man chosen to serve tables. Having such a revelation of the mind of Christ and of the depth and height of God, he could not be stopped in his experience. He went forward by leaps and bounds.

Beloved, there is a race to be run; there is a crown to be won; we cannot stand still! I say unto you, be vigilant! Be vigilant! "Let no man take your crown!"

You Are a Privileged Person

You can experience a supernatural union, a divine relationship, a power that will keep you alive to the fact that God makes everything subject to you when you reign with Christ Jesus.

I am reminded of the time Jesus raised Lazarus from the dead. Everyone at the tomb was filled with unbelief, and Jesus wept because of their unbelief. Jesus could not weep because Lazarus was dead, because he was the resurrection life. But their unbelief moved him to groan in his spirit, and he wept.

The sequel to that glorious triumph was a great union with his Father. He said to his Father, "I thank thee that thou hast heard me. And I knew that thou hearest me always: but because of the people which stand by I said it, that they may believe that thou hast sent me" (John 11:41, 42). Oh, the blessedness of the truth!

1 John 5:15 moves me tremendously. If I know he hears me, then I know that I have the petition that I desired of him. Knowing there is no power in the world that can take this truth away from you, you are privileged to go into the Holiest of Holies, through the Blood of the Lamb.

Glory to God!

-85-

Receiving Heavenly Riches

When Jesus becomes Lord of your affections and Lord of your will, all your desires and plans are subject to him. The Holy Spirit reveals Jesus in such a mighty way that he becomes Lord. And then when he becomes Lord, your desires, your wishes, your plans of life are ordered by the Lord.

God has given me a great mission, as you know, all over the world. The Lord has mightily blessed me, but God knows I do not glory in that. I want him to always be Lord of my life.

The truth of Matthew 16:19, that God will give us power to bind and loose, comes to me continually. Wherever I go, I emphasize this truth, to bring it into the hearts of the people, because I see that there is so much more for us in the divine order of God.

Do you desire that God may have his way through you? Now, beloved, I wonder if you have this clear knowledge that you belong to God. Would you like to be weighed down today with heavenly riches? Dare you believe that those hands of yours are holy hands? We lift up holy hands unto the Lord. Dare you, will you in the name of Jesus lift your hands up for God and pray?

> *Sweet will of God, still fold me closer,*
> *Till I am wholly lost in Thee.*
> *- Leila Morris*

Receiving God's Best

I want you to read 2 Corinthians 3. In this chapter, we have one of those high water marks of the very deep things of God in the Spirit. I believe that the Lord will reveal to us these truths as our hearts are open and receptive to the Spirit's leadings. Let not that man think that he shall receive anything of the Lord except along the line of spiritual revelation. For there is nothing that will profit you, except that which denounces or brings to death the natural order, that the supernatural plan of God may be revealed in you.

May the Lord of hosts camp round you today with songs of deliverance, that you may see the glories of his grace in a new way. For God hath not brought us into "cunningly devised fables," but, in these days, he is rolling away the mist and clouds that we may understand the mind and will of God.

If we are going to get the best that God has for us, there must be a spiritual desire, an open ear, an understanding heart. The veil must be lifted. We must see the Lord glorified in the midst of us. We must clearly see that we are not going to be able to understand these mysteries that God is unfolding to us only on the lines of being filled with the Spirit. We must see that God has nothing for us on the old lines. The new plan, the new revelation, the new victories are before us. All carnal things, and evil powers, and spiritual wickedness in high places must be dethroned.

꩜ ꩜ ꩜

The Life-giving Word

What an ideal position we are in as the sons of God now being manifested, now the glory is being seen, now the work is becoming an expressed purpose in life till the old life has ceased in them. How truly this position was shown forth in the life of Paul when he said, "I am crucified with Christ: nevertheless I live; yet not I, but Christ liveth in me: and the life which I now live in the flesh I live by the faith of the Son of God, who loved me, and gave himself for me" (Galatians 2:20).

Beloved, God would have us see that man is perfected only as the living Word abides in him. Jesus Christ is the express image of God, and the Word is the only factor that works in you and brings forth these glories of identification between you and Christ.

We may begin at Genesis, going right through the Pentateuch and the other Scriptures, and be able to rehearse them, but unless there is the living factor within us, they will be a dead letter. "The letter killeth, but the Spirit giveth life" (2 Corinthians 3:6).

We only know how to pray as the Spirit prayeth through us. The Spirit always brings to us the mind of God; he brings forth all our cries and needs; he takes the Word of God and brings our hearts and minds and souls, with all their need, into the presence of God. The Spirit prays according to the will of God, and the will of God is all in the Word of God.

A Heart Filled with God

L et us look at 2 Corinthians 3:3, a verse that rightly divides the word of truth: "Forasmuch as ye are manifestly declared to be the epistle of Christ ministered by us, written not with ink, but with the Spirit of the living God; not in tables of stone, but in fleshy tables of the heart."

May God help us to understand this truth, for it is out of the heart that all things proceed. When we have entered in with God, into the mind of the Spirit, we have found that God ravishes our hearts ["to be overcome with emotion and especially with joy or delight"—**Webster's New American Dictionary**].

When I speak about the fleshy tables of the heart, I mean the inward life. Nothing is so sweet to me as to know that the heart yearns with compassion. Eyes may see, ears may hear, but you may be immovable on the lines of love and compassion unless you have an inward cry where "deep calleth unto deep." When God gets into the depths of our hearts, he purifies every intention of our thoughts, and fills us with his own joy.

When Moses received the tables of stone on which the commandments were written, God made Moses' face to shine with great joy. Deeper than that, more wonderful than that are God's commandments written in our hearts; the deep movings of eternity rolling in, and bringing God in. O beloved, may our God, the Holy Spirit, have his way today in thus unfolding the grandeurs of Christ's glory.

How the Holy Spirit
Makes a Difference

I notice that many people fall short of God's rest because of unbelief. "For unto us was the gospel preached, as well as unto them: but the word preached did not profit them, not being mixed with faith in them that heard it" (Hebrews 4:2).

The last time I was in Wellington, I met people who had been Christians for years, but who were filled with unbelief. They will not accept the right way of the Lord. They break bread, but they will not tow the line. God save us from such a position.

Now it is unbelief, nothing else; but when the Holy Spirit comes, then unbelief is moved away, and they are humble, broken-hearted, thirsty, and they want God. May God keep us humble and hungry for the living Bread. God is showing me that you cannot have this blessed power without becoming hungry.

I pray God the Holy Spirit, that you will search your hearts and the Word, and see if you have received this Spirit. What is it? The Holy Spirit. When we are filled with the Holy Spirit, we are filled with the life of the Spirit, that which we call "unction," revelation, force.

I want to give you a very important point about the Holy Spirit today. The Holy Spirit is the only power that manifests the Word in the body of Christ. "For the Word of God is quick and powerful, and sharper than any two-edged sword, piercing even to the dividing asunder of soul and spirit, and of the joints and marrow, and is a discerner of the thoughts and intents of the heart" (Hebrews 4:12). May God help us.

⁂ ⁂ ⁂

-90-

Speaking as the Spirit Gives Utterance

I want to call your attention to Paul's writings to the church at Corinth where he shows a distinction between the Old and New Testaments.

"Who also hath made us able ministers of the New Testament; not of the letter, but of the Spirit; for the letter killeth, but the Spirit giveth life. But if the ministration of death, written and engraved in stones, was glorious, so that the children of Israel could not steadfastly behold the face of Moses for the glory of his countenance, which glory was to be done away, how shall not the ministration of the Spirit be rather glorious? For if the ministration of condemnation be glory, much more doth the ministration of righteousness exceed in glory" (2 Corinthians 3:6-9).

We cannot define, separate, or deeply investigate and unfold this holy plan of God unless we have the life of God, the thought of God, the Spirit of God, and the revelation of God. The Word of truth is pure, spiritual, and divine. People who are spiritual can only be fed on spiritual food. The message must be direct from heaven, red hot, burning, living. It must be truly "Thus saith the Lord," because you will speak only as the Spirit gives utterance, and thus you will always be giving forth fresh revelation. Whatever you say will be fruitful, elevating the mind, lifting the people, and all the people will want more.

–91–

Living in the Spirit

In John's Gospel, the Lord Jesus says he does not speak or act of himself: "The words that I speak unto you I speak not of myself but the Father that dwelleth in me, he doeth the works" (John 14:10).

We must know that the baptism of the Holy Spirit immerses us into an intensity of zeal and into the likeness of Jesus. We will be pure metal, so hot for God that we travel like oil from vessel to vessel.

This divine life of the Spirit will let us see that we have ceased from ourselves, and God has begun his work in us. The natural life has to die completely, because there is no other plan for a baptized soul—only to be dead indeed. We must live in the Spirit, must realize all the time that we are growing in that same ideal of our Master, in season and out of season, always beholding the face of the Lord Jesus. Old things are done away. "For even that which was made glorious, had no glory in this respect, by reason of the glory that excelleth. For if that which is done away was glorious, much more that which remaineth is glorious" (2 Corinthians 3:10, 11).

Thank God, the very doing away with the old law only fixes his commandments in our hearts more deeply than ever before. For out of the depths, we cry unto God, and in the depths has he cast out uncleanness and revealed his righteousness within. May God lead you every step in his divine life.

꒰⭢ ꒰⭢ ꒰⭢

-92-

Full Dependence on God

What a privilege to care for the flock of God, to be used by God to encourage his people, to help stand against the manifold trials that affect the needy. What a holy calling! We each have our own work, and we must do it so that boldness may be ours in the day of the Master's appearing and so that no man take our crown. As the Lord encourages us, we have that which can encourage others. There must be a willingness, a ready mind, a yielding to the mind of the Spirit. There is no place for the child of God in God's great plan except in humility. God can never do all he wants to do—all that he came to do through the Word—until he gets us to the place where he can trust us and where we are in abiding fellowship with him in his great plan for the world's redemption.

We have this illustrated in the life of Jacob. It took God twenty-one years to bring Jacob to the place of contrition of heart, humility, and brokenness of spirit. God even gave him power to wrestle with strength. Jacob foolishly thought he could manage after all—until God touched his thigh, making him know that he was mortal and that he was dealing with immortality (see Genesis 32:24-30).

> *He brought me out of the miry clay,*
> *He set my feet on the Rock to stay,*
> *He puts a song in my soul today,*
> *A song of praise, hallelujah.*
> *- Henry L. Gilmour*

The Necessity of Humility

In Mark 5:25, there is the story of a woman who had suffered many things of many physicians and had spent all that she had, and was not getting better, but rather growing worse. She said, "If I may but touch his clothes, I shall be whole." She came to know her need.

Our full cupboard is often our greatest hindrance. It is when we are **empty** and **undone** and come to God in our nothingness and helplessness that he picks us up.

> *The Great physician now is near*
> *The sympathizing Jesus;*
> *He speaks the drooping heart to cheer;*
> *Oh! hear the voice of Jesus.*
> *- William Hunter*

Peter says, "All of you be subject one to another, and be clothed with humility; for God resisteth the proud, and giveth grace to the humble. Humble yourselves therefore under the mighty hand of God, that he may exalt you in due time" (1 Peter 5:5-6).

Look at the Master at the Jordan River, submitting himself to the baptism of John, then again submitting himself to the cruel cross. Truly, angels desire to look into these things, and all heaven is waiting for the man who will burn all his bridges behind him and allow God to begin a plan in righteousness; so full, so sublime, beyond all human thought, but according to the revelation of the Spirit.

—94—

He Cares for You

The Apostle Peter urges us to depend on someone other than ourselves: "Casting all your care upon him." Why? He gives us the reason: "For he [Jesus] careth for you" (1 Peter 5:7)

> *He careth for you,*
> *He careth for you;*
> *Through sunshine or shadow,*
> *He careth for you.*
> *- Author Unknown*

Yes, he cares! We sometimes forget this. If we descend into the natural, all goes wrong, but when we trust him and abide beneath his shadow, how blessed it is. Oh, the times I have experienced my helplessness and nothingness, and casting my care upon him, have proved he cares!

Verse eight tells us to be sober and vigilant. What does it mean, to be sober? It is to have a clear knowledge that in yourself, you are powerless to manage; but by resting in faith, you will know God is near to deliver at all times. The adversary's opportunity comes when you try to open your own door. Our thoughts, words, acts, and deeds must all be in the power of the Holy Ghost. Oh, yes, we have need to be sober.

Not only have we need to be sober, but also to be vigilant, with an ability to judge, dissect, and balance things that differ. You need to be filled with the Spirit, but in addition, you need a "**go forth**," with a knowledge that God's holy presence is with you.

❧ ❧ ❧

-95-

Steadfast in Faith

When we have had experiences in certain areas, we are able to counsel others. Peter gives us good advice under the anointing of the Spirit: "Your adversary, the devil, as a roaring lion, walketh about, seeking whom he may devour, whom resist steadfast in the faith" (1 Peter 5:8-9). We must resist in the hour when, by Satan's wiles, we may be bewildered and we are almost swept off our feet. We must resist when darkness is upon us to such a degree that it seems as if some evil thing had overtaken us. Our resistance is to be steadfast in the faith. He that keepeth Israel neither slumbers nor sleeps. God covers us, for no humanity can stand against the powers of hell.

Tongues with Interpretation: "The strongholds of God are stronger than the strength of man and he never faileth to interpose on behalf of his own."

Peter acknowledges that there is suffering: "After ye have suffered" (verse 10). Yes! But these sufferings are not to be compared to the eternal glory that is to be revealed to us.

In verse 11, we are instructed to give God all the glory. What does it mean for it all to be realized in my case? That I live for his glory, that there be no withdrawal, no relinquishing, no looking back, but going on, on, on, for his glory now and forever, until, as Enoch, we walk with God, and are not, for God will take us.

ॐ ॐ ॐ

–96–

Meeting God at Bethel

Jacob had deceived in every way. He had deceived to get his birthright, to get his cattle. He was a deceiver. Truly, the devil had a big play with Jacob, but, praise God, there was one thing that Jacob knew: He knew that God had fulfilled his promise.

After Jacob had cheated his brother Esau out of the birthright, he fled to his mother's family at Haran (Genesis 28:5). On the way to Haran, Jacob had an encounter with God, which changed his life. He called the place Bethel, which means the place of prayer, the house of God (Genesis 28:19).

In Bethel, God let Jacob see the wonderful ladder that reached from earth to heaven with angels ascending and descending. It was the earthly entering heaven.

Later, God brought him right back to this same place (Genesis 35:1-15). It made no difference how he had wandered. It did not matter to God. God swore to him, and he brought him back.

Oh, it is marvelous how God meets us in our distresses. When the cry comes from broken hearts, then God comes. Have you been there yet? How many times have you tried and failed?

Oh, my friend, let God come, and the whole thing will be at an end. Let God come! Will you?

Oh, it is so lovely to me to know that God in his mercy never faileth.

※ ※ ※

The Compassionate Jesus

Beloved, I believe that God would be pleased for you to read from the fifth chapter of St. Mark's Gospel, from verse 21 to the end of the chapter. This is a wonderful passage; in fact, all of God's Word is wonderful. It is the Word of Life, and it is the impartation of the life of the Savior.

Jesus came to give eternal life, and he also came to make our bodies whole. I believe that God, the Holy Spirit, wants to reveal the fullness of redemption through the power of Christ's atonement on Calvary, until every soul shall get a new sight of Jesus, the Lamb of God.

He is lovely. He is altogether lovely. Oh, he is so beautiful! You talk about being decked with the rarest garments, but, oh, he could weep with those that weep. He could have compassion on all. There were none that missed his eye. When he was at the pool, he knew the impotent man and understood his case altogether. And when he was at Nain, the compassion of the Master was so manifested that it was victorious over death. Do you know that love and compassion are stronger than death? If we touch God, the Holy Spirit, he is the ideal principle of divine life for weaknesses. He is health. He is joy.

Jesus is the living substance of faith. You can be perfectly adjusted by the blood of Jesus. We must believe in the Spirit's power and see our blessed position in the risen Christ.

−98−

The Breath of God

A fter the risen Lord appeared to his disciples, they received a marvelous experience: "He breathed on them, and saith unto them, Receive ye the Holy Ghost" (John 20:22).

God would have you know that he is waiting to impart life. Oh, if you would only believe! Oh, you need not wait another moment. Just now, receive the impartation of life by the power of the Word. Do you not know that the Holy Ghost is the breath of Heaven, the breath of God, the Divine impartation of power that moves in the human, and which raises from the dead and quickeneth all things?

One of the things that happened on the Day of Pentecost in the manifestation of the Spirit was a mighty, rushing wind. The Third Person was manifested in wind, power, might, revelation, glory, and emancipation. Glory to God!

This wind was the life of God coming and filling the whole place where they were sitting. And when I say to you, "Breathe in," I do not mean merely breathe; I mean breathe in God's life, God's power, the Personality of God. Hallelujah!

This is why I am on this platform—because of this holy, divine Person who is breath, life, revelation. His power moved me, transformed me, sent me, revised the whole of my position.

꙳ ꙳ ꙳

The Truth Will Set You Free

Yℴou cannot find anywhere that God ever failed. Now this unfailing God wants to bring us into that blessed place of faith, changing us into a real substance of faith till we are so likeminded that whatever we ask in faith, we receive. As a result, our joy becomes full.

Hear what God said to Abraham in Genesis 12:1-3, and then see how Abraham acts. He was among his own people and his own kindred, and God said to him, "Come out, Abraham, come out!" And Abraham obeyed and came out, not knowing where he was going.

You say, "He was the biggest ass that ever God had under his hands." You will never go through with God on any lines except by believing him. It is, "Thus saith the Lord" every time; and you will see the plan of God come right through when you dare to believe. He came right out of his own country, and God was with him. Because he believed God, God overshadowed him.

I want, by the help of God, to lead you into the truth, for nothing but the truth can set you free; truth can always do it. Jesus gave an important promise not only to his disciples, but also to you: "Ye shall know the truth, and the truth shall make you free" (John 8:32).

Here is our assurance: If God covers you with his righteousness, it is impossible for anything to happen to you contrary to the mind of God.

ॐ ॐ ॐ

Lord, I Do Believe

A certain woman, which had an issue of blood twelve years ... came in the press behind, and touched his garment (Mark 5:25, 27).

This poor woman was in an awful state. She spent all her money on physicians and was "nothing bettered, but rather grew worse."

This poor woman said, "If I may touch but his clothes, I shall be whole" (verse 28). No doubt, she thought of her weakness, but faith is never weak. She may have been very weary, but faith is never weary. The opportunity had come for her to touch him, and "straightway the fountain of her blood was dried up; and she felt in her body that she was healed of that plague."

Jesus knew that virtue had gone out of him, and he said, "Who touched me?" The woman was fearful and trembling, but she fell down before the Lord and told him the truth. And he said unto her, "Daughter, thy faith hath made thee whole; go in peace, and be whole of thy plague" (verse 34).

The opportunity comes to you now to be healed. Will you believe? Will you touch him? There is something in a living faith that is different from anything else. I have seen marvelous things accomplished just because people said, "Lord, I believe."

> *Lord, I believe, I believe!*
> *Savior, raise my faith in Thee,*
> *Till it can move a mountain;*
> *Lord, I believe, I believe!*
> *All my doubts are buried in the fountain.*
> *- Author Unknown*

Without Condemnation

God wants us to be holy, and he wants us to be filled with a power that keeps us holy. He wants us to have a revelation of what sin and death are, and what the Spirit and the life of the Spirit are.

Take a look at the first two verses of Romans 8: "There is therefore now no condemnation to them which are in Christ Jesus, who walk not after the flesh but after the Spirit. For the law of the Spirit of life in Christ Jesus hath made me free from the law of sin and death."

"No condemnation." This is the primary word to consider today because it means so much it has everything within it. If you are without condemnation, you are in a place where you can pray through, where you have a revelation of Christ. For him to be in you brings you to a place where you cannot but follow the divine leadings of the Spirit of Christ; and where you have no fellowship with the world.

I want you to see that if you love the world, you cannot love God, and the love of God cannot be in you; so, God wants a straight cut. Why does God want a straight cut? Because if you are "in Christ," you are a "new creation"— you are in him—you belong to a new creation in the Spirit. Therefore, you walk in the Spirit and are free from condemnation. That is his promise today!

࿐ ࿐ ࿐

-102-

Filled with God

God wants all of his people to be targets, to be lights, to be like cities set on a hill which cannot be hid; to be so "in God" for the world's redemption that they may know you belong to God. That is the law of the Spirit. What will it do? The law of the Spirit of life in Christ Jesus will make you free from the law of sin and death (Romans 8:2).

Sin will have no dominion over you. You will have no desire to sin, and it will be as true in your case as it was in Jesus' case when he said, "Satan cometh, but findeth no thing in me." Satan cannot condemn; he has no power. His power is destroyed, as we see in Romans 8:10. What does it say? "If Christ be in you, the body is dead because of sin; but the Spirit is life because of righteousness."

To be filled with God means that you are free: full of joy, peace, blessing, endurement, strength of character, molded afresh in God, and transformed by his mighty power till you *live*, yet not you, but "another lives in you," manifesting his power through you as sons of God.

Jesus saith, "Be not afraid, only believe" (Mark 5:36). The people in whom God delights are the ones who rest upon his Word without wavering. God has nothing for the man who wavers, for "let him that wavereth expect nothing from God" (James 1:6).

꙰ ꙰ ꙰

-103-

Reigning with Christ—Now and Forever

Today, let us look at two laws: the law of the Spirit of life in Christ Jesus and the law of sin and death. The first law makes you free from the second. The law of sin and death is still in you, but it is dead. You are just the same person, only quickened (made alive)—the same flesh, but it is dead. You are a new creation—a new creature! Created in God afresh after the image of Christ.

Now, beloved, some people come into line with this, but do not understand their inheritance and go down; but instead of you being weak and falling, you must rise triumphantly over it.

You might say, "Show me the law." I will, God helping me. It is found in Romans 7:25, the last verse: "I thank God through Jesus Christ our Lord. So then, with the mind I myself serve the law of God; but with the flesh the law of sin."

Is it a sin to work? No, it is not a sin to work. Work is ordained by God. It is an honor to work. I find that there are two ways to work. One way is working in the flesh, but the child of God should never allow himself to come into the flesh when God has taken him in the Spirit. God wants to show you that there is a place where you can live in the Spirit and not be subject to the flesh. Live in the Spirit till sin has no dominion. "Sin reigned unto death, even so grace reigns through righteousness unto eternal life by Jesus Christ our Lord" (Romans 5:21).

-104-

Something Better than Adam Enjoyed

When I think of the Garden of Eden, when Adam and Eve had fellowship with God, I wonder if there is anything greater.

Yes, redemption is greater. How? Anything that is local is never so great. It was wonderful when God was in the Garden with Adam, but that was local. The moment a man is born again he is free, and lives in heavenly places. He has no destination except living in glory. God wants you to come into this glorious redemption, not only for the salvation of your soul, but also for your body—to know that it is redeemed from the curse of the law—to know that you have been made free—to know that God's Son has set you free. Hallelujah! Free from the law of sin and death! How is it accomplished?

Here are the master verses: "For what the law could not do, in that it was weak through the flesh, God, sending his own Son in the likeness of sinful flesh, and for sin, condemned sin in the flesh, that the righteousness of the law might be fulfilled in us who walk not after the flesh, but after the Spirit" (Romans 8:3, 4). Righteousness fulfilled in us!

I tell you there is a redemption—there is an atonement in Christ—a personality of Christ to dwell in you. There is a God likeness for you to attain—a blessed resemblance of Christ in you, if you will believe the Word of God. The Word is sufficient for you; eat and devour this living Word of God.

Jesus Destroys the Works of the Devil

Jesus was manifested to destroy the works of the devil. God so manifested his fullness in Jesus that he walked this earth glorified and filled with God. In the first place, he was with God and was called "the Word." In the second place, he and God became one, so much so that in their operation people said it was "God;" and then the cooperation of oneness was so manifest that there was nothing done without the other. They cooperated in the working of power.

Then you must see that before the foundation of the world, this plan of redemption was all completed and set in order before the fall. Notice, too, that this redemption had to be mighty to redeem us all so perfectly. There should be no lack in the whole plan.

Let us see how it comes about. First, Jesus became flesh; then he was filled with the Holy Spirit; then he became the voice and the operation of the Word, by the power of God, through the Holy Spirit. He became "the Authority."

Are you confident in his redemption today? If you will only believe it, you are secure. For there is a greater power in you than in all the world. Hallelujah!

As you go about your activities today, may this little chorus inspire you to believe God:

> *Only believe!*
> *Only believe!*
> *All things are possible—*
> *Only believe.*

-106-

God Gives Us New Life

L et us look at the law of sin—the law that is without the Holy Spirit. Here is a person who has never known regeneration, being led captive by the devil at his will. There is no power that can convert this person except the Blood of Jesus. Men try without the Blood; science tries without it; all have tried without it; but all are left shaking on the brink of hell—without it. Nothing can deliver you but the blood of the Lamb. We are free from the law of sin and death only by the Spirit of life in Christ Jesus (Romans 8:2). Then we can have clean hearts, pure lives.

The carnal life is not subject to the will of God, neither indeed can be. Carnality is selfishness—uncleanness. It cannot be subject to God; it will not believe; it interferes with you; it binds and keeps you in bondage; but, beloved, God destroys carnality; he destroys the work of the flesh. How? By a new life, which is so much better—by a peace, which passes all understanding; by a joy, which is unspeakable and full of glory. The full story, though, cannot be told. Everything that God does is too big to tell. His grace is too big. His love is too big. His salvation is too big to be told. It is so vast, mighty, and wonderful. Why, it takes all heaven to contain this story! But the good news is that God gives us the power to understand what we need to know.

❧❧ ❧❧ ❧❧

-107-

Made Alive by the Spirit

Have you experienced the fact that our God is an abundant God? His love is far exceeding and abundant above all that we can ask or think. After ye were illuminated—glory to God you were quickened [made alive] by the Spirit, and now are looking forward to a day of rapture when you will be caught up and lifted into the presence of God. You cannot think of God on any small line. God's lines are beyond measure—wonderful and glorious.

Let me touch an important point. Christ Jesus has borne the Cross for us so there is no need for us to bear it. He has borne the curse, for "cursed is every one that hangeth on a tree" (Galatians 3:13). The curse covered everything. When Christ was in the grave, the Word says that he was raised from the dead by the operation of God through the Spirit. He was made alive by the Spirit in the grave, and so the same Spirit dwelling in you shall quicken your mortal bodies.

Jesus rose by the quickening power of the Holy Ghost: "But if the Spirit of him that raised up Jesus from the dead dwell in you, he that raised up Christ from the dead shall also quicken your mortal bodies" (Romans 8:11).

What does it mean? Now, it is no longer a mortal body you have, but the promise of immortality in the resurrection. Then he will quicken your mortal body.

-108-

The Benefits of Divine Healing

If you will allow Jesus to have control of your bodies, you will find his Spirit will quicken you [make you alive] and loose you from bondage. He will show you that it is the mortal body that has to be quickened. Talk about divine healing! The Scriptures are full of it.

Everyone that is healed by the power of God—especially believers—will find their healing an incentive to make them purer and holier. If divine healing was given only to make you whole, it would be worth nothing. Divine healing is a divine act of the providence of God coming into your mortal body and touching it with Almightiness.

Could you remain the same? No! Like me, you will go out to worship and serve God. That is why I have gone around the world—because of the healing of God in this mortal body. I don't go to build new orders of things. God wants me to preach so that everyone who hears me should go back to his own home with the energy and power of God and the revelation of Christ.

The moment you yield yourself to God, the Bible becomes a new Book; it becomes revelation so that we have the fullness of redemption going right through our bodies in every way—filled with all the fullness of the Godhead bodily.

Filled with God! Yes, filled with God,
Pardoned and cleansed and filled with God.
Filled with God! Yes, filled with God,
Emptied of self and filled with God!
- Author Unknown

Requirements for Service

And in those days when the number of the disciples was multiplied, there arose a murmuring of the Grecians against the Hebrews, because their widows were neglected in the daily ministration. Then the twelve called the multitude of the disciples unto them, and said, 'It is not reason that we should leave the Word of God and serve tables. Wherefore, brethren, look ye out among you seven men of honest report, full of the Holy Ghost and wisdom, whom we may appoint unto this business …' and the saying pleased the whole multitude: and they chose Stephen, a man full of faith and of the Holy Ghost, and Philip [and ×ve others] (Acts 6:1-5).

Here we see that the disciples were hard pressed to keep up with all the ministries of the early church. The things of natural order could not be attended to, and many were complaining concerning the neglect of their widows. The disciples therefore decided upon a plan, which was to choose seven men to do the work—men who were "full of the Holy Ghost."

What a divine thought! No matter what kind of work they faced, however menial it may have been, the person chosen must be filled with the Holy Spirit. The plan of the church was that everything, even of natural order, must be sanctified unto God, for the church had to be a Holy Spirit church.

Beloved, God has never ordained anything less!

❧ ❧ ❧

-110-

Have You Received the Holy Spirit?

No matter on what continent I preach, no matter what else may happen, first and foremost there is one thing I stress: Have you received the Holy Spirit since you believed? Are you filled with divine power?

This is the heritage of the church, to be so endued with power that God can lay his hand upon any member at any time to do his perfect will.

There is no stopping in the Spirit-filled life: We begin at the cross, the place of ignominy, shame, and death, and that very death brings the power of resurrection life. And then, being filled with the Holy Spirit, we go on "from glory to glory." Let us not forget that being baptized in the Holy Spirit means there must be an ever-increasing holiness.

> *The power! The power!*
> *Gives victory over sin*
> *and purity within;*
> *The power! The power!*
> *The pow'r they had at Pentecost.*
> *- Charles F. Weigle*

How the church needs divine unction—God's presence and power so manifest that the world will know it.

An Ordinary Man Becomes Mighty

God has privileged us in Christ Jesus to live above the ordinary human place of life. Those, who want to be ordinary and live on a lower plane, can do so. But as for me, I will not! For the same unction, the same zeal, the same Holy Spirit power is at our command as was at the command of the apostles. We have the same God that Abraham and Elijah served, and we need not come behind in any gift or grace. There should be a manifestation of the gifts as God may choose to use us.

Stephen was an ordinary man who became mighty under the Holy Spirit's anointing until he stood supreme, in many ways, among the apostles: "And Stephen, full of faith and power, did great wonders and miracles among the people" (Acts 6:8).

As we go deeper in God, he enlarges our conception and places before us a wide-open door; and I am not surprised that this man, chosen to serve tables, was afterwards called to a higher plane. Oh, that we might be awakened to believe his Word, to understand the mind of the Spirit, for there is an inner place of whiteness and purity where we can see God. Stephen was just as ordinary a man as you and I, but he was in the place where God could so move upon him that he, in turn, could move all before him. He began in a most humble place, and ended in a blaze of glory. Beloved, dare to believe Christ!

Enemies of God's Servants

As you progress in this life of the Spirit, you will find that the devil will begin to get restless, and there will be a stir in the synagogue. It was so with Stephen. Any number of people may be found in the "synagogue," who are very proper in a worldly sense—always correctly dressed, the elite of the land, welcoming into the church everything but the power of God.

This is what God says about them: "Then there arose certain of the synagogue, which is called the synagogue of the Libertines, and Cyrenians, and Alexandrians ... disputing with Stephen, and they were not able to resist the wisdom and the Spirit by which he spake" (Acts 6:9, 10).

The Libertines could not stand the truth of God. They became full of wrath in the very place where they should have been full of the power of God, full of love divine and reverence for the Holy Spirit. They rose up against Stephen, this man "full of the Holy Ghost."

Beloved, if there is anything in your life that in any way resists the power of the Holy Ghost and the entrance of his Word into your heart and life, drop on your knees and cry aloud for mercy! When the Spirit of God is brooding over your heart's door, do not resist him but open your heart to the touch of God. He will answer and fill your heart to overflowing.

God Gives Courage to His Faithful Servants

You will find that no matter what the place or situation, there is always a moving when the Holy Spirit has control. That's what happened when Stephen was hauled into the council for preaching Christ (Acts 6, 7). Those who opposed him were brought under conviction by the message of Stephen, but they resisted. They did anything and everything to stifle that conviction. Not only did they lie, but they also got others to lie against this man, who would have laid down his life for any one of them. Stephen was used to heal the sick, perform miracles, and yet they brought false accusations against him.

What effect did it have on Stephen? "And all that sat in the council, looking steadfastly on him, saw his face as it had been the face of an angel" (Acts 6:15).

Something had happened in the life of this man who was chosen for menial service yet became mighty for God. How was it accomplished in him? It was because his aim was high; faithful in little, God brought him to full fruition. Under the inspiration of divine power by which he spoke, the council could do nothing but listen—even the angels listened, as with holy prophetic utterance he spake before that council.

Do you need courage today for an important responsibility? God will meet your need as you seek him and remain faithful as Stephen did.

-114-

Forgiving One's Enemies

As you look at Acts 6 and 7, you'll see Stephen, speaking under the inspiration of the Holy Spirit, and the men of this council being "pricked to the heart" rise up as one man to slay him.

From his place of helplessness, Stephen looked up and said, "Behold, I see the heavens opened, and the Son of Man standing at the right hand of God" (Acts 7:56).

Is that the position Jesus took after his ascension? No! He went to sit at the right hand of the Father. But in behalf of Stephen, the first martyr, the man with that burning flame of Holy Spirit power, God's Son stood up in honorary testimony of him who, called to serve tables, was faithful unto death.

But is that all? No! I am so glad that it is not all. As the stones came flying at him, pounding his body, crashing into his bones, striking his temple, mangling his beautiful face, what happened? How did this scene end? With that sublime, upward look, this man chosen for an ordinary task, but filled with the Holy Spirit, was so moved upon by God that he finished his earthly work in a blaze of glory, magnifying God with his last breath. Looking up into the face of the Master, he said, "'Lord, lay not this sin to their charge.' And when he had said this, he fell asleep" (Acts 7:60).

Friend, it is worth dying a thousand deaths to gain that Spirit. My God! What a divine ending to the life and testimony of a man who was chosen to serve tables. He remained faithful unto death and even forgave his enemies in his dying breath.

❧ ❧ ❧

Power for Every Emergency

L et us take a look at 1 Corinthians 12:1. "Concerning spiritual gifts, brethren, I would not have you ignorant." Now when the Holy Spirit says that, he expects us to understand what the gifts are, and he wants us to understand that the Church may be able to profit thereby.

Now, read verses 6 and 7: "There are diversities of operations, but it is the same God which worketh all in all. But the manifestation of the Spirit is given to every man to profit withal." Everyone who has received the Holy Spirit has within himself great possibilities and unlimited power. He also has great possessions, not only of things, which are present, but also of things to come. The Holy Spirit has power to equip you for every emergency.

The reason people are not thus equipped is that they do not receive him and do not yield to him; they are timid and doubt, and in the measure that they doubt, they go down. But if you yield to his leadings and do not doubt, it will lead you to success and victory; you will grow in grace and will have not only a controlling power, but you will have a revealing power of the mind and purposes which God has for you.

> *Marching on, marching on,*
> *For Christ count everything but loss!*
> *And to crown him King*
> *Toil and sing*
> *'Neath the banner of the cross!*
> *- D. W. Whittle*

A Faith That Will Cast Out Unbelief

I see where all things are in the power of the Holy Spirit, and I must not fail to give you the same truth.

We must remember that we have entered into the manifestation of the glory of God, and in that are great power and strength. Many people might be far ahead of where they are today, but they have doubted. If by any means, the enemy can come in and make you believe a lie, he will do so. We have had to struggle to maintain our standing in our salvation, for the enemy would beat us out of that if possible. It is in the closeness of the association and oneness with Christ where there is no fear, but perfect confidence all the time. The child of God need not go back a day for his experience, for the presence of the Lord is with him, and the Holy Spirit is in him and in mighty power if he will believe. I see, too, that we should stir up one another and provoke one another to good works.

If we find that there is unbelief in us, we must search our hearts to see why it is there. Where there is a living faith, there is no unbelief, and we go on from faith to faith until it becomes as natural to live there as can be. But if you try to live faith before you are just, you will fail, for "the just shall live by faith." And when you are just, it is a natural consequence for you to live by faith. It is easy; it is joyful; it is more than that; it is our life and spiritual inheritance.

Taking Victory Through the Holy Spirit

Today you might have a broken heart; you might have a longing for something to strengthen you in conditions that exist in your home and a power to make these conditions different. Maybe you are unequally yoked together.

Beloved, you have a mighty power that is greater than all natural power. You can take victory over your home, and your spouse, and children, but you must do it in the Lord's way. Suppose you do see many things that ought to be different; if it is your cross, you must take it and win the victory for God. It can be done, for greater is he that is in you than all the power of hell. I reckon that any person filled with the Holy Spirit is equal to a legion of devils any day.

A man in Glasgow got up and said, "I have power to cast out devils." A man full of devils got up and came to him, and the bragging man did everything he could, but could not cast out the devils. Do you want to cast out devils? Make certain it is the Holy Spirit who does it.

The secret is to allow the Holy Spirit to dwell within you, and then you will adore Jesus. Other things must be left behind; I must adore him.

Getting a Fix on the Word of God

A person who is baptized with the Holy Spirit has a Jesus mission. He knows his vocation and the plan of his life. God speaks to him so definitely that there is no mistaking it. Thank God for the knowledge which fixes me so solidly upon God's Word that I cannot be moved from it by any storm that may rage.

The revelation of Jesus to my soul by the Holy Spirit brings me to a place where I am willing, if need be, ***to die on what the word says***. Look at the three Hebrew children, for example, who refused to bow to the king's gods and said, "We are not careful to answer thee in this matter. If it be so, our God whom we serve is able to deliver us from the burning fiery furnace, and he will deliver us out of thine hand, O King. But if not, be it known unto thee, O King, that we will not serve thy gods, nor worship the golden image which thou hast set up" (Deuteronomy 3:16-18).

When a person is quickened by the Spirit, he never moves toward or depends upon natural resources. Even though the furnace is heated seven times hotter is of no consequence to the person who has heard the voice of God; the lions' den has no fear for the person who opens his windows and talks to his Father. People who live in the Spirit are taken out of the world in the sense that they are kept in the world without being defiled by the evil of the world.

༃ ༃ ༃

-119-

Remaining Faithful

We see a wonderful example in Elisha as one who sensed God's call and had a willingness to obey. Elisha left his oxen, the plow, and everything; and he burned all bridges behind him (see 1 Kings 19:20, 21). Beloved, the Lord has called you. Are you separated from the old things that will hold you back?

As Elisha traveled with Elijah, he heard and saw the wonderful things of his ministry. The time came when his master said to him, "I am going to Bethel today, I want you to remain here." "Master," Elisha said, "I must go with you." Other people knew something about it for they said to him, "Do you know the Master is going to be taken away from you today?" He said, "Hold your peace, I know it." Later on the master said, "I want to go on to Jericho; you stay here." But Elisha says, "No, I will not leave thee." God had revealed to Elisha that Elijah would be leaving this earth. Elisha did not want to miss anything (see 2 Kings 2).

Perhaps God is drawing you to do something; you feel it.

If you see zeal in somebody else, reach for it; it is for you. God wants all of the members of his body joined together, to remain faithful to their call just as Elisha did. If you see others who have failed to go on with God, perhaps he is calling you to speak and to pray and to encourage them.

God needs everyone to carry out his plan.

Anointed to Serve

On the day that God would translate Elijah and give the prophet's young assistant Elisha his mantle, the two walked together as usual. When they came to the Jordan River, Elijah switched his mantle over the river, and they passed over on dry ground. No doubt Elisha said, "I must follow his steps." And when they had gone over, the old man said, "You have done well, you would not stay back; what is the real desire in your heart? I feel I am going to leave you; ask what you like now before I leave you." "Master," he says, "I have seen all that you have done; Master, I want twice as much as you have" (2 Kings 2:9). (I believe it is the faint-hearted that do not get much.)

As they continued up the hill, down came the chariot of fire, nearer and nearer, and when it lands, the old man jumps in. Elisha said, "My father, My father," and down came the mantle. Elisha returned to the waters as an ordinary man, but with the knowledge that he possessed the mantle. Then he said, "Where is the God of Elijah?" (2 Kings 2:14). And he put his feet down. When you put your feet down and say you are going to have a double portion, you will get it.

What have you asked for? Are you satisfied to go on in the old way when the Holy Spirit has come to give you an unlimited supply of power, and he says, "What will you have?" We see Peter so filled with the Holy Spirit that his shadow falling on sick people healed them. He asked for power and he got it.

What do you want? Are you asking for a double portion today?

No Longer You, but the Holy Spirit

For as much as ye are zealous of spiritual gifts, seek that ye may excel to the edifying of the church (1 Corinthians 14:12).

The Bible is the Word of God, and it is most important that when we read it, we do so with purpose of heart to obey its every precept. We have no right to open the Word of God carelessly or indifferently. I have no right to come to you with any message unless it is absolutely in the perfect order of God.

We have a great need today. It is that we may be supplied with revelation according to the mind of the Lord; that we may be instructed by the mind of the Spirit; that we may be able to rightly divide the Word of Truth; that we may not be novices, seeing that the Spirit of the Lord has come to us in revelation. We ought to be alert to every touch of divine and spiritual illumination.

We should carefully consider what the apostle said to us, "Grieve not the Holy Spirit of God, whereby ye are sealed unto the day of redemption" (Ephesians 4:30).

I trust that you shall not come behind in any gift. You say, "I have asked; do you think God will be pleased to have me ask again?" Yes, go before him; ask again. And you can go forth today, not in your own strength, but in the Holy Spirit.

੨☙ ੨☙ ੨☙

-122-

God's Will in Chastening

Here is a principle we don't want to accept, but it is God's Word: "Now no chastening [discipline or correction] for the present seemeth to be joyous, but grievous; nevertheless afterward it yieldeth the peaceable fruit of righteousness unto them which are exercised thereby" (Hebrews 12:11).

When God performs surgery on us, it might be painful, but the wise saint will remember that to those he chastens, "it yieldeth the peaceable fruit of righteousness."

Therefore, let him do with you what seemeth good to him, for he has his hand upon you and will not willingly take it off till he has performed the thing he knows you need. So if he comes with a fan, be ready for the fan. If he comes with chastisement, be ready for chastisement. If he comes with correction, be ready for correction. Whatever he wills to do, let him do it, and he will bring you to the land of plenty.

If he chastens you not, if you sail placidly along without incident, without crosses, without persecutions, without trials, remember that "if ye be without chastisement, whereof all are partakers, then are ye bastards and not sons" (Hebrews 12:8). Therefore, "Examine yourselves, whether ye be in the faith" (2 Corinthians 13:5). And never forget that Jesus wants you to follow him, and wants you to have a clear ring in your testimony.

Oh, it is worth the world to be under the power of the Holy Spirit!

֍ ֍ ֍

Gifts that Will Meet Every Need

Now there are diversities of gifts, but the same Spirit. And there are
differences of administrations, but the same Lord. And there are
diversities of operations, but it is the same God which worketh
all in all. But the manifestation of the Spirit is given to every man
to pro×t withal (1 Corinthians 12:4-7).

The variation of humanity is tremendous. Faces are different,
so is physique. Your whole body may be so tempered that
one particular gift would not suit you at all while it would suit
another person.

So the Word of God deals here with varieties of gifts, meaning that
these gifts perfectly meet the condition of believers everywhere.
That is God's plan. Not one person would be led to claim all gifts.
Paul said that you need not come behind in any gift. God has for
you wonderful things beyond what you have ever known.

My friend, I am no good without the Holy Ghost. The power of the
Holy Ghost loosed my language. I could not tell a story because
I was bound. I had plenty of thoughts, but no language. But, oh,
after the Holy Ghost came!

I had a great desire after gifts. So the Lord caused me to see that
it is possible for every believer to live in such holy unction, such
divine communion, such pressed-in measure by the power of the
Spirit that every gift can be his.

Coveting the Best Gifts

Wherever I have traveled, I have found a vast and appalling unconcern among God's people about possessing spiritual gifts. Ask a score of saints chosen at random from almost any assembly, "Have you any of the gifts of the Spirit?" and the answer will be, "No." The answer comes in a tone and manner that conveys the thought that the saint is not surprised at not having the gifts, that they do not expect to have any of them, and do not expect to seek for them. Is not this terrible when this living Word exhorts us specifically to "covet earnestly the best gifts" (1 Corinthians 12:31)?

So that the gift might be everything and in evidence, we must determine that we live only for his glory. He works with us, we work with him, cooperative, working together. This is divine. Surely, this is God's plan.

God has brought you to the banquet and he wants your hunger satisfied. We are in a place where God wants to give us visions. We are in a place where our Lord in his great love bends over us with kisses. Oh, how lovely the kiss of Jesus, the expression of his love!

Oh, come, let us seek him for the best gifts, and let us strive to be wise and rightly divide the Word of truth, giving it forth in power, that the church may be edified and sinners may be saved.

-125-

Divine Utterances

Peter has a word for us today: "For we have not followed cunningly devised fables, when we made known unto you the power and coming of our Lord Jesus Christ, but were eye witnesses of his majesty. For he received from God the Father honour and glory, when there came such a voice to him from the excellent glory" (2 Peter 1:16, 17).

Sometimes people wonder why it is that the Holy Spirit is always expressing himself in words. It cannot be otherwise. You could not understand it otherwise. You cannot understand God when you see believers shaking, and yet at times, shakings might be in perfect order. But you can always tell when the Spirit moves through utterances. The utterances magnify God. The Holy Spirit has a perfect plan. He comes right through every person who is so filled, and brings divine utterances that we may understand what the mind of the Lord is.

May I take you to three expressions in the Bible about the glory? "Therefore my heart is glad, and my glory rejoiceth" (Psalm 16:9). His glad heart produced glory. Now turn to Psalm 108:1: "O God, my heart is fixed; I will sing and give praise, even with my glory." You see, when the body is filled with the power of God, then the only thing that can express glory is the tongue. Glory is presence, and the presence always comes by the tongue, which brings forth the revelations of God.

"Out of the abundance of the heart the mouth speaketh" (Matthew 12:34).

꒒꒥ ꒒꒥ ꒒꒥

-126-

Bringing Heaven to Earth

Virtue is to be transmitted, and glory expressed. So God, by filling us with the Holy Spirit, has brought into us this glory, that out of us may come forth the glory. The Holy Spirit understands everything Christ has in the glory and brings through the heart of man God's latest thought.

The world's needs, our manifestations, revivals, and all conditions are first settled in heaven, then worked out on the earth. So we must be in touch with God Almighty to bring out on the face of the earth all the things that God has in the heavens. This is an ideal for us, and God help us not to forsake the sense of holy communion, entering into the prayer closet in privacy, that publicly he may manifest his glory.

We must see the face of the Lord and understand his workings. There are things that God says to me that I know must take place. It does not matter what people say. I have been face to face with some of the most trying moments of men's lives, when it meant so much if I kept the vision and held fast to what God had said. A person must be in an immovable condition, and the voice of God must mean to him more than what he sees, feels, or what people say. He or she must have an originality born in heaven, transmitted or expressed in some way. We must bring heaven to earth.

❧❧ ❧❧ ❧❧

God Has Given Us All Things

L et us turn to 2 Peter 1:3, "According as his divine power hath given unto us all things that pertain unto life and godliness, through the knowledge of him that hath called us to glory and virtue."

Oh, this is a lovely verse. There is so much depth in it for us. It is as divinely appointed for you as when the Holy Spirit was upon Peter, and he brings it out for us. It is life to me; it is like breath; it moves me. I must live in this grace. "According as his divine power"—there it is again—"hath given unto us all things that pertain unto life and godliness."

> *Deeper, deeper in the love of Jesus*
> *Daily let me go;*
> *Higher, higher in the school of wisdom,*
> *More of grace to know.*
> *- Charles P. Jones*

Oh, what wonderful things he has given us "through the knowledge of him that hath called us to glory and virtue." You cannot get away from him. He is the center of all things. He moves the earth, transforms beings, can live in every mind, plan every thought.

God is available for us all the time. "For he hath said, 'I will never leave thee, nor forsake thee.' So that we may boldly say, 'The Lord is my helper, and I will not fear what man shall do unto me'" (Hebrews 13:5, 6).

꒜ ꒜ ꒜

–128–

Maintaining a Close Walk with God

Many people have lost the glory of God that they once knew because they have been taken up with the natural. If we are to accomplish in the Spirit the thing God has purposed for us, we can never turn again to the flesh. If we are Spirit-filled, God has cut us short and brought us into relationship with himself, joined us to another, and now he is all in all to us.

You may have a vision of the Lord at all times, whether you are in a railway train, or in a bus, or walking down a street. A Christian ought to have such an unction of the Holy Spirit as to realize at any moment, whether in the presence of others or alone, that he is with God. He can have a vision in public transportation, even if others are standing in front of or behind him; or he can have a vision if he is there alone.

> *I've heard the voice of my Savior*
> *telling me still to fight on;*
> *He promised never to leave me,*
> *never to leave me alone.*
> *- Author Unknown*

Nehemiah stood before the king because of trouble in Jerusalem which had almost broken his heart. He was sorrowful, and it affected his countenance; but he was so near to God that he could say, "I have communed with the God of heaven." And if we believers are to go forth and fulfill God's purpose with us, the Holy Spirit must constantly fill us and move upon us until our whole being is on fire with the presence and power of God.

Reaching God's Appointed Place

God is shaking the earth to its foundations, and making us understand a principle in the Scriptures that can free men and women, boys and girls from the natural order, and bring them into a place of holiness, righteousness, and the peace of God which passeth all human understanding. We must reach it. Praise God!

God brought us into his kingdom for a purpose. He wants us to grow, to advance in our Christian walk. You might say, "How shall I be able to get all that he has laid up for me?" Friend, I know only one way—a broken and contrite heart he will not despise.

What do you want today? Be definite in your seeking. God knows what you need, and that one thing is ready for you now. Set your minds that you will know today the powers of the world to come.

I have great love for my sons in England, great love for my daughter, Alice, who often travels with me. But that love is nothing in comparison with God's love toward us. God's love is desirous that we walk up and down the earth as did his Son—clothed, filled, radiant, with fire beaming forth from our countenance, setting forth the power of the Spirit, so that people jump into liberty.

"Ask and it shall be given you; seek, and ye shall find; knock, and it shall be opened unto you. For every one that asketh receiveth; and he that seeketh findeth; and to him that knocketh it shall be opened" (Luke 11:9, 10).

A Power Behind the Scenes

I think the best word you can ask today is the question Paul asked when Jesus appeared to him on the road to Damascus (Acts 9:6): "Lord, what wilt thou have me to do?" The greatest difficulty today is for us to be held in the place where it is God only—because it is so easy to get our own mind working. But, the working of the Holy Spirit is so different. I believe there is a mind of Christ, and we may be so immersed in the Spirit that we are all day asking, "What wilt thou have me to do?"

I used to think that if I could see God perform certain things, I would be satisfied, but I have seen greater things recently than I ever expected to see, and I am more hungry to see greater things yet. The great thing when believers come together in worship is to get us so immersed in God that we may see signs and wonders in the name of the Lord Jesus. If God has taken hold of us, we will be changed by his power and might. God has a plan to turn the world upside down and can do it when we are not in the way.

When I have been at my wit's end, and have seen God open the door, I have felt I should never doubt God again. I have been taken to another place that was worse still. There is no place for us, and yet a place where God is, where the Holy Spirit is just showing forth and displaying his graces. It is a place where we are always immersed in the Spirit. It is wonderful!

Friend, there is a power behind the scenes of your life that can move things. That is God's power, and it is for you today.

꒰꒱ ꒰꒱ ꒰꒱

Moving Mountains
Through the Spirit

I believe we have yet to learn how it would be with a church that truly understood the work of intercession. I believe God the Holy Spirit wants to teach us that it is not only people on the platform who can move things by prayer. The Lord can move things through people in the pew.

When I was in a little room at Bern, Switzerland, waiting for my passport, I found a lot of people, but I couldn't speak to them because I didn't know their language. So I got hold of three men and pulled them unto me. They stared, but I got them on their knees. Then we prayed, and the revival began. I couldn't talk to them, but I could show them the way to talk to someone else.

God will move upon people to make them see the glory of God just as it was when Jesus walked in this world. And I believe the Holy Spirit will do special wonders and miracles in these last days.

"Jesus answering saith unto them, 'Have faith in God. For verily I say unto you, That whosoever shall say unto this mountain, 'Be thou removed, and be thou cast into the sea,' and shall not doubt in his heart, but shall believe that those things which he saith shall come to pass, he shall have whatsoever he saith. Therefore I say unto you, What things soever ye desire, when Ye pray, believe that ye receive them, and ye shall have them'" (Mark 11:22-24).

Setting a Watch Over Our Tongue

As Jesus and the Twelve gathered together, he looked on them and said right into their ears, "One of you which eateth with me shall betray me" (Mark 14:18).

Jesus knew who would betray him. He had known it for many, many months. They whispered to one another, "Who is it?" None of them had real confidence that it would not be he. That is the serious part about it. They had so little confidence in their ability to face the opposition that was before them, and they had no confidence that they would not betray the Lord.

Jesus knew. He had talked to Judas many times, rebuking him, and telling him that his course would surely bring him to a bad end. He never had told any of his disciples who would betray him, not even John, who leaned on his breast.

Now if believers would set a watch on their tongue, it would purify the church. But I fear sometimes Satan gets the advantage and things are told before they are true. James wrote that no man in the natural can tame the unruly tongue (James 3:8). But I believe God wants to so sanctify us, so separate us, that we will have that perfection of love that will not speak ill of other believers, that will not slander other believers.

"Though I speak with the tongues of men and of angels, and have not charity [love], I am become as sounding brass, or a tinkling cymbal" (1 Corinthians 13:1).

An Essential Combination

And now abideth faith, hope, charity [love], these three; but the greatest of these is charity. Follow after charity, and desire spiritual gifts, but rather that ye may prophesy. For he that speaketh in an unknown tongue speaketh not unto men, but unto God: for no man understandeth him; howbeit in the Spirit he speaketh mysteries. But he that prophesieth and speaketh unto men to edi×cation, and exhortation, and comfort (1 Corinthians 13:13; 14:1-3).

When love is in perfect progress, other things will work in harmony, for prophetic utterances are of no value unless perfectly covered by divine love.

Jesus was so full of love to his Father and love to us that his love never failed to accomplish its purpose. It works in us and through us by the power of the Father's love in him. This is what must come into our lives.

Beloved, there is human language on the human plane, but that same language can be changed by spiritual power. That divine touch of prophetic utterance will never come except as you are filled with the Spirit. If you wish to do anything for God, do not miss the plan; you cannot afford to be on ordinary lines. You must realize that within you there is a power of the Spirit that is forming everything you require.

-134-

How to Set the Church on Fire

We enjoyed some wonderful experiences in the early days of the Christian Mission in England [later called Salvation Army]. I have never seen anything like it in my life. The power of God rested upon the worst characters, and they were saved. It reached every class. Drunkards were saved right and left; and the next day when they stood to testify, their testimony thrilled the place so that the power of God fell upon others, who in turn became witnesses to the salvation of Christ. There was no such thing as a building large enough to hold the work; the meetings were in open market places, and they put big wagons there for platforms.

I maintain that we are in a different and higher order than in those days, yet we lack. We have too much preaching and too little testifying. You can never keep a church on fire with a preacher every night preaching, preaching, preaching. The people become weary of preaching, but they never tire of the whole place being on fire.

Lord, send the old-time pow'r,
the Pentecostal pow'r
Thy floodgate of blessing on us
throw open wide!
Lord, send the old-time pow'r;
the Pentecostal pow'r
That sinners be converted
And thy name glorified!
- Charles H. Gabriel

In the Fullness of the Spirit

If you attend a Pentecostal meeting and sit through it unmoved, you are not in the Spirit, and dearth will fall on the church.

When the Holy Spirit comes in his fullness, he comes into a person to move him so that he knows he has to speak now in a different way. "When he, the Spirit of truth, is come, he will guide you into all truth" (John 16:13). The Holy Spirit is inspiration, revelation, manifestation, operation. When a man comes into the fullness of the Holy Spirit, he is in perfect order, built on a scriptural foundation.

I have failed to find any man who understood the 12th, 13th and 14th chapters of First Corinthians unless he had been baptized in the Holy Spirit. When a man gets baptized with the Holy Spirit, he speaks from a deep inward conviction, by the power of the Spirit, a revelation of that Scripture.

I often kneel before God thinking, "Now what is the burden of my heart?" The Lord knows more than I do about the burden, and the moment I kneel down, I lose all my English. I am in the presence of God, and he takes me right on to victory. Talk about this praying in the Holy Spirit, there is nothing like it! It is a secret between you and God.

-136-

Our Potential in God's Hands

Without a doubt, God wants to bring to our eyes and ears living realization of what the Word of God is, what he means through his Word, and what we may expect if we believe it. The Lord wishes to put before us a living fact, which shall by faith bring into action a principle, which is within our own hearts so that Christ can dethrone every power of Satan. It is only this truth revealed to our hearts that can make us so much greater than we thought possible. I believe there are volumes of truth contained in our own hearts; but there is the need of revelation, and we need to stir ourselves to understand the mightiness, which God has within us.

God has not accomplished something in us that should lie dormant, but he has brought within us a power, a revelation, a life that is so great, that I believe he wants to reveal the greatness of it.

Our potential accomplishments on a natural basis are limited to what God has for us on a spiritual basis. If man can accomplish much in the natural, what may we accomplish if we will take the revealed Word as truth and demonstrate it in force? The possibilities of a person in the hands of God! There is not anything you can imagine greater than what that person may accomplish.

〰 〰 〰

The Holy Spirit Is in Charge

For to one is given by the Spirit the word of wisdom; to another the word of knowledge by the same Spirit (1 Corinthians 12:8).

If the Spirit can stir you up today, you will come short in no gift. God wants you to see that we need not come behind in any gift, and he wants to bring us to a place where we will be on fire because of what he has called us to.

It is in the perfect will of God that we should possess the needed gifts, but there must be unity between God and you. When the gifts are in evidence, the whole church is built up, Christ being the head. Jesus said, "I come to do thy will, my God!" And as we surrender in that way, God will be delighted to hand to us the gift, which is necessary.

The more we realize that God has furnished us with a gift, the more completely we will be united with Jesus so that people will be conscious of him rather than of his gift.

Oh, beloved, if our ministry with the gift is not totally of the Holy Spirit and glorifies Jesus, it will all be a failure and come to naught. There was none so self-conscious as they who said, "In thy name we have cast out devils." They were so controlled by the natural and the thought that they had done it all, that God was not in it. But when he comes forth and does it, it is all right.

-138-

Singing in the Spirit

People who are baptized in the Holy Spirit can have a wonderful time in song. I have seen it, especially in England, and if we only understood it better, we should have greater chorals than ever were sung, far better than man ever made. I have heard singing in the Spirit with such rarity of music as I have never heard elsewhere, music from the deepest bass to octaves higher than you ever hear in the natural.*

All is in perfect harmony, and it makes you think of a big organ, only more massive, more beautiful. Everyone weeps and rejoices and is solemn in the presence of God, so that there is nothing in the flesh. The people are melted down at such times. I pray God we may all come to understand this in its fullness. Remember that when love is in perfect progress, other things will work in harmony.

Wigglesworth's friend and Triumphs of Faith *editor Carrie Judd Montgomery often reported unusual happenings in the early Pentecostal meetings. Nobody would forget the "Heavenly Dove" singing solos in unknown tongues through a woman at these meetings. She wrote in her autobiography, "Ofttimes the audience would be moved by the Spirit to chime in with all the parts of the heavenly chorus, and its volume and sweetness were so great that one would almost unconsciously look up expecting to see hosts of angels joining with us."* (Under His Wings, The Story of My Life, *214 [Oakland, California:* Triumphs of Faith, *1936].)*

꒰꒱ ꒰꒱ ꒰꒱

How to Have Good Success

"Ye have not chosen me, but I have chosen you, and ordained you that ye should go and bring forth fruit, and that your fruit should remain: that whatsoever ye shall ask the Father in my Name, he may give it you" (John 15:16).

God wants, by the power of the Spirit, to reveal unto us our position in Christ. We see Jesus foreshadowing blessings that were to come. Most of his ministry was a type of what the believer was to enter into. Let us see what God had in his mind to do through his Son for us. He wants us to be right up-to-date in everything, and the Spirit of the Lord shall be able to bring before our minds today what is the mind of the Spirit concerning us, so that we may step into all the privileges.

God wants a strong people. Remember the charge God gave Joshua (see Joshua 1). He said, "Be full of courage; be neither dismayed nor discouraged"—and then he gave him the charge. If God forecasts anything for you, he will give the power to carry it through. So, after he had given Joshua the word, he said, in effect, "Now it will depend upon your living, day and night, meditating upon the Word of God," and as you come into this blessed state of holy reverence for the Word of God, it will build you up also, and make you strong.

"Then thou shalt have good success," he told Joshua. In this state of grace, whenever Joshua put his foot down, he was not to let it slide back, but to put the other foot ready to go forward.

-140-

When God Ordains Us

What Jesus said to the disciples, he says to us. And if we can believe, God has ordained us—by the Holy Spirit to fill us and clothe us till we know we are the chosen of God. We are precious in his sight to bear the vessels of the Lord, to be not only co-workers with him, but to divide the powers of Satan.

This salvation is too big and great for any mind to take in. It is only the flash of eternity, the divine light of heaven, the Spirit of the living God with that infinite mind that can flash into the caverns of the human soul. Then we see the whole heaven, and are changed by his power till there is not a weak point, not an unbelieving attitude; because the Word has so changed us that we are a perfect pattern of the new covenant of Christ.

The ordination was finished, but there was a lack of power. The credentials were all right, but the power was not there. "I have chosen you, and ordained you, that ye should go and bring forth fruit, and that your fruit should remain: that, whatsoever ye shall ask of the Father in my name, he may give it you" (John 15:16). I believe God wants us to know that our fruit has to remain. Beloved, we should recognize that our prayers are in vain unless we really expect what we ask to be granted to us.

꙰ ꙰ ꙰

-141-

The Life-giving Word

There is a time when the preaching of the Word has no value to the hearers. Look at Hebrews 3:2. "The Word preached did not profit them, not being mixed with faith in them that heard it." But today may God give us the Word of faith, and you shall know for a fact that there is a great change in you. The Word quickens the preacher, the hearer, and everybody.

One day in Toronto, at the close of a service, I saw one of the leaders rush out as though something had happened. When I got home, I found he had brought a man to me who was in a very strange way. He was a man of fine physique and looked quite all right, but his nerves were shattered, and he asked me if I could do anything for a man who had not slept properly for three years.

The sleepless man said, "I have a business, a beautiful ranch and a home—it is all going. My whole nervous system is in an awful state, and unless something happens, I shall lose everything." He stood in front of me and asked for help. I said, "Go home and sleep." He remonstrated, but I insisted that he must obey my command and *go*! He went home, got into bed, fell asleep, and slept all night. In fact, he told me afterwards that his wife had to wake him.

He came along to see me again, and said, "I have slept all night; I am a new man. The whole situation is changed now" The Word giveth life, and God wants it to be so alive in you that you will be moved as it is preached.

-142-

In Time of Emergency

If we are filled with the Spirit, we are ready for every emergency. We know Paul walked close to God because of what happened in Acts 20. There the people became so hungry for God, they were still listening to Paul after midnight. As Paul poured forth the Word of God, a young man fell down from the third loft and died. Paul, in the same glorious fashion as always, went down and embraced him and pressed the very life from himself into the young man. He brought him back to life. Always equipped for emergency, blessed, holy equipment by God!

Living in the Holy Spirit, walking in the divine likeness, having no confidence in the flesh, but growing in the grace and knowledge of God, and going on from one state of glorious perfection unto another state of perfection—that is it. You cannot compare the Holy Spirit to anything less, but something more, than ever you thought about. That is the reason the Holy Spirit has to come into us to give us divine revelations for the moment. The person who is a "partaker of the divine nature" has come into a relationship where God imparts his divine mind for the comprehension of his love and of the fellowship of his Son.

We are only powerful as we know that source; we are only strong as we behold the Beatitudes and all the wonderful things and graces of the Spirit.

-143-

Seek and You Shall Find

In Luke 8:41, we read about a man by the name of Jairus who came to Jesus. I would like you to think about the sorrow this man and his wife suffered. They have a sick daughter who seemingly is beyond help. They have heard quite a lot about Jesus, and I fancy I hear the woman say to her husband, "There's only one thing left; if you could see Jesus, our daughter would live."

My friend, if you see Jesus today, you will live. God can so reveal him to your hearts that, while you hear his Word, you can see Jesus. The Holy Spirit will show you the way of salvation, and oh, it is a wonderful way. Think about him. Did you ever think about him? Talk about love! There is no love like his! His love has never changed. He loved us while we were yet sinners, and then he died for us. Nobody is saved when they are good; they are always saved when they are bad. God has a way of revealing our hearts to us, and when we see ourselves as sinners, he applies the balm.

Is it possible for anybody to seek Jesus and not find him? Is it? Jairus went to seek Jesus. It is not possible for you to seek Jesus today without finding him. They that seek him find him just the same as this man did. Glory to God! There is nothing in the world so lovely as the knowledge that God reaches out, and those who seek him find him, and he finds them.

Jesus Shows His Compassion

It is impossible to know the Word of God without knowing that he will meet you just as he met a sick woman in Luke 8. As Jesus and his disciples traveled along a certain road, a great pack of people surrounded them. Then we read about the sick woman in verse 43.

I can just imagine some of those people who had seen Jesus say to this woman, "Oh, if you had only been with us today! We have seen such wonderful things; we are sure you would have been healed. We thought about you." And as they told this woman all about what Jesus had done that day, she said, "Oh, if I was only able to touch his garment, I believe I should be whole, also."

Is it possible? This woman was worse than she had been twelve years before. Beloved, I tell you it is impossible for anyone to have an inward desire of seeing and meeting with Jesus, but what they will both see and feel and **know** him.

God's Word is true. People who seek Jesus will find him. And this woman was so moved by these stories that day by day, she longed to see Jesus. And, glory to God, the day came! There was a great cry: All the people were thronging and surrounding him on all sides and rushing out of the houses and saying, "Oh, there he is!" The woman pushed her way in and **touched him**, and the touch did it. God wants reality in your hearts today, bringing you into the same determination to touch **Jesus**!

A Deluge of the Spirit

The baptism in the Holy Spirit is nothing less than the third Person of the Blessed Trinity coming down from glory. It is the Executive Spirit of the Triune God who causes us to yearn with compassion, as Jesus did; to travail as he travailed; to mourn as he mourned; to groan as he groaned.

It cannot be otherwise with you. You cannot experience the baptism in the Holy Spirit along a merely passive line. It does not come that way. But, glory be to God, it does come. Oh, that God might bring from our hearts the cry for such a deluge of the Spirit that we could not get away till we were ready for him to fulfill his purpose in us and for us.

If there is anything I know about this baptism it is this: that it is such a force of conviction in my life that I am carried, as it were, through the very depths of it. Sometimes we have to think; at other times, we have not time to think, and it is when we are at our wits' end that God comes and brings deliverance. When you are at your wits' end, and you throw yourself on the omnipotent power of God, what a wonderful transformation there is in a moment.

Peter and John were hauled into the council because a lame man was healed, and they were preaching in Jesus' name. Were they ready to quit? No! Read how they prayed after they were released: "Lord, behold their threatenings, and grant unto thy servants, that with all boldness they may speak thy word" (Acts 4:29). You will discover the mighty deluge they experienced by reading verses 30 and 31. Hallelujah!

-146-

The Power of the Word

While Jesus was on the way to Jairus' house (see Luke 8), he healed the woman who suffered with an issue of blood. But just when everyone was beginning to see that Jesus was everything they needed and wanted, into the midst of the throng came the devil. Yes, he always comes at a busy time.

Four or five people rushed from the house of Jairus right into the presence of Jesus, took hold of Jairus, and said, "Look here! Do not trouble Jesus any more; your daughter is dead. He can do nothing for a dead daughter." But Jesus said, "Believe only!" (Luke 8:50).

God help us today to believe. Only to believe! Oh, what blessing it is if we believe! Allow God to divest you of everything, beloved. Allow the Word to sink into your heart. Allow it to drive away everything else. There is eternal life if you will believe. You are "heirs and joint heirs" with him.

If you are not saved, you can be saved by the power of the faith I am speaking to you about. Only believe. You cannot save yourself. The more you try in your own strength, the more you get fixed up; but, oh, if you will believe, God will save you, he will do it. You can know today that God loves you and will save you. Bless the Lord, O my soul, and all that is within me, bless his Holy Name!

As They Went, They Were Healed

Sometimes we are tested on the lines of faith. For twenty-five years, Abraham believed God. He said to him, "Thy wife shall have a son." Every year his wife grew weaker. He saw the wrinkles and her puny weak condition. Did he look at it? No—he looked at the promise. For twenty-five years God tested him, but he gave glory to God, and considered neither Sarah's body nor his own and as he did so, God said, "Yes, Abraham."

Listen to what the Word says: "Now it was not written for his sake alone ... but for us also ... if we believe on him that raised up Jesus our Lord from the dead; who was delivered for our offenses, and was raised again for our justification" (Romans 4:23-25).

All who believe are blessed along with faithful Abraham. God wants to show us that nothing is impossible to those who believe. I would like God to reveal himself to you today. People ask me, "How long will it be before I am healed?" And I ask, "How long will it be before you believe God?"

I would like you to see the story of the ten lepers in Luke 17:11-19. When they saw Jesus, they shouted, "Jesus, Master, have mercy upon us." And he shouted and answered them, "Go, show yourselves to the priests." Was it an impossibility? Yes, humanly speaking, but the lame were helped by those that were not lame, and the blind by those that could see, and the whole regiment went their way, and **as they went, they were healed**. As they believed, they were healed. Hallelujah!

These signs shall follow them that believe upon his name—go, preach the gospel, then will he confirm the same.

≈ ≈ ≈

-148-

Not My Plan, but His

I want to draw your attention to Acts 26:12-19, where we are told of the light from Heaven and the voice, which arrested Paul on his way to Damascus. Here we read of his conversion and of the commission given to him to go unto the Gentiles to turn them from darkness to light, and from the power of Satan unto God. Here too we read that he "was not disobedient unto the heavenly vision" (verse 19).

You might remember reading in Acts 9, that for three days after this vision, Paul was blind; he was in a broken-hearted condition, I suppose. And then God had him. It is a wonderful thing when God gets you. You are not much good for anything until he does.

Well, Paul had first to come to this time of crying, weeping, contrition, brokenness, yieldedness. He had done all he could in the natural, but the natural had only brought him to a broken place, to blindness, to helplessness, and this had to come out of Paul's life before he could have the life of God.

When we have altogether parted with our own, as it were, then there is a possibility of God's likeness being made manifest in us, of the water of life filling us. This experience not only fertilizes our own life, but it also *flows from us as a river* that will touch others. When God is in the plan, everything works mightily and harmoniously. I pray that at all times I should cease from anything except that thing which God wants to bring out. Not my plan, but his.

෧෧ ෧෧ ෧෧

A Yielded, Obedient Life

L et us think about the Pentecostal experience and the fullness of the Spirit, and of what God is able to do through us when we are yielded to him. We gather in his name to kindle one another with a holier zeal than has ever possessed us before. I believe there is a greater need for us now than ever before. There are more broken spirits in our land than there have been for a long time past, and no one can meet the need today but a person filled with God.

Just as the sun by its mighty power brings certain resources to nature, so I believe in the power of God in the human soul—the power filling it with himself is capable, by living faith, of bringing about what otherwise could never be accomplished. May God prepare to minister to others through his Spirit.

There are so many wonderful things about a life filled with the Holy Spirit that one almost feels like a machine, one that never stops speaking of those. There are so many opportunities and such great forces that can come from no other place. When Jesus would not make bread for himself, he made bread for thousands. And when I will not do anything for myself, then God will do something for me, and then *I will gladly do anything for him that he wants*. That is the purpose of the baptism in the Holy Spirit. It creates yielded and obedient men and women.

A Burning in the Soul

In his helplessness and brokenness on the road to Damascus, Paul cried, "Lord, what wilt thou have me to do?" (Acts 9:6). That cry reached to heaven. As a result, there came Ananias, a holy man, touched with the same fire and zeal that filled his Master. He laid his hands upon Paul and told him that Jesus had sent him to restore his sight and that he would be filled with the Holy Spirit.

When God moves a person, his body becomes akin with celestial glory all the time, and he says things as he is led by the Holy Spirit who fills him. When we are filled with the Holy Spirit, we go forth to see things accomplished that we could never see otherwise.

Paul had a vision. There is always a vision in the baptism of the Spirit. But visions are no good except as I make them real, except as I claim them, except as I make them my own. If your whole desire is to carry out what the Spirit has revealed to you by vision, it will surely come to pass.

Many people lack power because they do not allow the fire to burn continuously. There must be a continuous burning on the altar. The Holy Spirit's power in a person is meant to be an increasing force, an enlargement. God's work is never of a diminishing type. He is always going on. You must not stop in the plains; there are far greater things for you on the hilltops than in the plains. Hallelujah!

-151-

Only in the Name of Jesus

Paul seemed to be so filled with the Holy Spirit that people could bring aprons and handkerchiefs, and he could send them forth with healing power (Acts 19:12). I can imagine these people looking on and saying, "But it is all in the name. Don't you notice that when he sends the handkerchiefs and the aprons he says, 'In the name of the Lord Jesus, I command evil to come out'?"

These people thought, "It is only the name, that is all that is needed." And so seven men said, "We will do the same." These seven sons of Sceva were determined to do as Paul was doing. They came to one who was demon-possessed and said, "We adjure you by Jesus whom Paul preacheth" (Acts 19:13). The demon said, "Jesus I know, and Paul I know, but who are ye?" (verse 15). Then this evil power leaped upon them and tore their clothing from off their backs, and they went out naked and wounded.

It was the right name, but they did not understand it. Oh, that God would help us understand the name! It is the name, but you must understand there is the ministry of the name; there is something in the name that makes the whole world charmed. It is the Holy Spirit back of the ministry; it is the knowledge of him; it is the ministry of the knowledge of him; and I can understand it is only that.

> *Yesterday, today, forever,*
> *Jesus is the same;*
> *All may change, but Jesus never!*
> *Glory to His name.*
> *- A. B. Simpson*

Letting God Direct Your Path

A common mistake today is to think that everything ought to be done *in a tremendous hurry*. With God it is not so. God takes plenty of time, and he has a wonderful way of developing things as he goes along. Nothing that you undertake will fail, if only you do not forget what he has told you—and if you act upon it. Notice how different Joshua and Caleb were from the other ten spies. The others returned from spying out the Promised Land with a negative report, saying the enemy would defeat God's people. Joshua and Caleb responded, "If the Lord delights in us, then he will bring us into this land, and give it us; a land floweth with milk and honey. Only rebel not ye against the Lord, neither fear ye the people of the land" (Numbers 14:8, 9).

That is the way of people who are baptized in the Holy Spirit. They are no longer living in the natural; they are directed by the Spirit; they are turned into new people.

Where are you fixed? Is God the Holy Spirit arranging things for you or are you arranging things according to your own plan? A person filled with the Holy Spirit has ceased to be, in a sense. He has come to a rest. He has come where God is working—to a place where he can "stand still and see the salvation of the Lord." Such a person has ceased from his own works and abilities and associations. He will not trust his own heart; he relies only on the omnipotent power of the Most High.

ॐ ॐ ॐ

Keeping in Touch

The person baptized with the Holy Spirit will always **keep in touch with his Master** wherever he may be. He has no room for anything that steps lower than the unction that was on his Master, or for anything that hinders him from being about his Master's business. If you are baptized in the Holy Spirit, you have no spiritual food apart from the Word of God. You have no resources but those that are heavenly. You have been "planted" with Christ, and have "risen with him." You are "seated with him in heavenly places;" your language is a heavenly language, and your source of inspiration is a heavenly touch; God is enthroned in your whole life, and you see things "from above," and not from below.

I have seen people filled with the Holy Spirit who used to be absolutely helpless; and when the power of God took their bodies, they became like young people instead of old withered people through the power of the Holy Spirit; but now I am going to show you the reason. The Word of God is quick and powerful. Paul said, "You hath he quickened" (Ephesians 2:1). And that quickening makes us alive, and it is powerful: "For the weapons of our warfare are not carnal, but mighty through God to the pulling down of [Satan's] strongholds" (2 Corinthians 10:4).

A New Power

In the fourth chapter of James, we read that some asked amiss that they might consume it on their own lusts. There is a need for spiritual gifts, and God will reveal to you what you ought to have, and you ought never to be satisfied until you receive it.

When I received the new birth at eight years of age, it was so precious and lovely; I have never lost the knowledge that God has accepted me since that time. Beloved, there was a work that God wrought in me when I tarried for the baptism in the Holy Spirit. It is a wonderful work. I was in a strange position; I had testified to having received the baptism for sixteen years and had the anointing of the Spirit; I could not speak without it. My wife would come to me and say, "The people are waiting for you to come out and speak to them." I would say, "I cannot and will not come without the anointing of the Spirit."

I can see now I was calling the anointing "the baptism." But when the Holy Spirit came into my body, God took this tongue, and I spoke as the Spirit gave utterance, which brought perfect satisfaction to me. I then began to reach out as the Holy Spirit showed me. When he comes in, he abides.

It is important that we realize we can do nothing of ourselves. Being clothed with the power of God, we will not operate in the natural man in a sense. But as we go forth in this power, things will take place as they took place in the days of the disciples.

Jesus said, "Every one that asketh receiveth" (Matthew 7:8). What are you asking for? What is your motive?

۞ ۞ ۞

Paul, Our Wonderful Example

L et us look at the Apostle Paul's wonderful vision while he was
on the road to Damascus (Acts 9). I want you to see how
carefully the Lord deals with him in the more detailed account in
Acts 26: "But rise, and stand upon thy feet: for I have appeared
unto thee for this purpose, to make thee a minister and a witness
both of these things which thou hast seen, and of those things in
which I will appear unto thee" (verse 16).

See how carefully the Lord works? He shows Paul the vision as
far as Paul can take it, and then he says there are other "things in
which I will [again] appear unto thee." Did he ever appear unto
Paul after that? Certainly he did. But Paul never lost this vision; he
kept it up, so to speak.

What was there in the vision that held him in such close association
with Jesus Christ that he was ready for every activity to which he
was led by the Holy Spirit? There were certain things he had to do.
Look, for instance, at Galatians 1:15, 16. "When it pleased God,
who separated me from my mother's womb, and called me by his
grace, to reveal his Son in me, that I might preach him among the
heathen; immediately I conferred not with flesh and blood."

What Paul received came through the Holy Spirit, not through
even the words of the apostles. His obedience to God's call
and commission is a good example for us. "Therefore I was not
disobedient to the heavenly vision" (Acts 26:19), and "I conferred
not with flesh and blood" (Galatians 1:16).

꩜ ꩜ ꩜

-156-

Spiritual Riches for Everyone

In Ephesians 3:20 are words, which no human man could ever think or plan with pen and ink. They are so mighty, so of God when it speaks about his being able to do all things: "exceeding abundantly above all that we ask or think."

The mighty God of revelation!

The Holy Spirit gave these words of grandeur through Paul to stir our hearts, to move our affections, to transform us altogether. This is ideal! This is God. Shall we teach them? Shall we have them? Oh, they are ours.

God has never put anything on a pole where you could not reach it. He has brought his plan down to man; and if we are prepared today, oh, there is so much more for us!

I feel sometimes God has given us just as much as we can digest, yet there are such divine nuggets of precious truth held before our hearts, it makes you understand that there are yet heights, and depths, and lengths, and breadths of the knowledge of God laid up for us. We might truly say,

> *My heavenly bank, my heavenly bank,*
> *The house of God's treasure and store.*
> *I have plenty in here; I'm a real millionaire.*
> *- Author Unknown*

Never to be poverty-struck anymore. An inward knowledge of a greater bank than ever the Rothchilds or any other rich men have known about. It is stored up, nugget upon nugget, weights of glory, expressions of the invisible Christ to be seen by men. Glory!

–157–

Seeking God First

A man in Toronto who had been healed of a nervous condition asked me, "Can you get my money back? My business back? Can you get my house put in order again?"

I knew this man was a perfect stranger to salvation and knew nothing about it, but I said, "Yes—everything. You shan't lose a thing. You be at the meeting tonight."

He was in the audience, and I preached the gospel, which is the power of God unto salvation; and as I preached, this man became very uneasy. As I preached on, he became more and more restless; it seemed as though he could not bear to sit in his seat. As I gave the altar call, he rushed forward for salvation and for healing. But he fell in the aisle. He could not get away from God's call. Oh, it is lovely.

When this man fell, I said, "Nobody touch him! No one speak to him—keep your hands off the man; God has him in hand." God made a fine job of him; he began worshiping the Lord, became a wonderful citizen, was delivered out of the clutches of Satan, and got everything squared up.

Oh, when God begins to move, everything is soon in order. "Seek ye first the kingdom of God and his righteousness, and all these things shall be added unto you" (Matthew 6:33).

꙰ ꙰ ꙰

Revealing the Glory of God

It was a necessity that Jesus should live with his disciples for three years, and walk in and out amongst them and manifest his glory, and show it forth day by day. Those men already believed in God, but this Messiah had continued, day by day, to bring himself into their vision, into their minds, into their very nature. He had pressed himself right into their lives to make them successful after he had ascended to heaven. He had shown them how wonderfully and gracefully and peacefully he could move the crowds.

Do you remember the story of the man sick of palsy who was lowered through the roof? The house was crowded with people who waited to hear and see Jesus. So the men had to take the sick man to the roof and lower him into Jesus' presence.

The way to the cities was so pressed with the people who were following Jesus and his disciples, that he and they could hardly move, but he always had time to stop and perform some good deed on the journey. Do you think the disciples noticed this? Yes, and what he had brought home to the minds and hearts of the disciples was that he was truly the Son of God. They could not accomplish their preordained ministry until he had proved that to them, and until he had soared to glory. They could only manifest him to others when he had imparted his life into the very core of their nature. Others were astonished and would confess, "We never saw things like this."

Today in place of Jesus walking with us as he did with the disciples, we can be clothed with the Holy Spirit. Then we, too, can manifest his glory.

꒰ꔷ ꒰ꔷ ꒰ꔷ

The Touch That Changes

When the woman with the issue of blood touched Jesus, he turned around and said, "Who touched me?" (Luke 8:45). And Peter said, "That's a nice thing to say, why all the people are leaning upon you; everybody's leaning on you." "Yes," he said, "But somebody touched me."

Oh, there's a difference! You may be crippled all your life; but one atom of faith will do it. So Peter asked, "What do you mean, Lord?" And he said "Someone has touched me!" And then the woman turned around and said, "Yes, it was me; but I am so different now; the moment I touched you, I was made whole!"

"Ah!" he answered her, "Go in peace, thy faith hath made thee whole." Notice that it was not "thy touch," but "thy faith." Her faith had healed her. And that is what it takes today, a living faith.

His Word was the authority of faith. "If thou canst believe." Believe what? Believe what the Word says. They came and asked him, saying, "Tell us how we may work the works of God." He said, "This is the work of God, that ye **believe** him whom God hath sent." "This is the work of God." O, beloved, I should be a poor man without the Word of God, but I am rich.

Oh, the Word of God—the Living Word—the precious, precious, Word of God. Jesus said, "Search the Scriptures, for in them ye think ye have eternal life: and these are they which testify of Me" (John 5:39). Hallelujah!

❧ ❧ ❧

All Things Are Possible

I met a young woman who for six years could not drink normally or she would choke. Her body was weak and the ordeal had affected her mind.

I knew it was the power of Satan. But the young woman was willing to trust the one who has power over Satan. "You will be free, and you will drink as much as you want as soon as I am done with you, if you will believe. As sure as you are standing there, you will drink as much as you want."

So I said to her, "Now, do you dare to believe?" "Yes, I believe that in the name of Jesus you can cast the evil power out." I then laid my hands upon her, and I said, "***It's done; you drink***." She went laughing and praising God. She drew the first glass of water and drank.

"Mother! Father! Brother!" she said, "I've drunk one glass!" There was joy in the house.

What healed her? It was the living faith of the Son of God. Oh, if we only knew how rich we are, and how near we are to him at the fountain of life! "All things are possible to him that believeth" (Mark 9:23). Peter told Eneas, "Arise and make thy bed. And he arose immediately" (Acts 9:34). What did it? A life clothed with the Spirit.

Tongues and Interpretation: "The living water is falling and making manifest the Christ mission to those who will enter in by a living faith. Nothing can hinder the life-flow to those who believe, for all things are possible to them that believe."

Can He Count on You?

When you are born of God, or when God is born into you, and you become a quickened soul to carry out the convictions of the life of the Spirit of God—instantly on the threshold of your new birth comes a vision of what your life is to be.

The question is whether you dare go through with the vision. Will you hold on to the very thing the Holy Spirit brought to you? Will you determine never to lose sight of it, but press on in a life of devotion to God and of fellowship and unity with him?

My passion is that God shall endue you with such an unction and cry that you will not be satisfied until you feel the members of your body on fire with a Spirit-kindled unity. It is not too late to put on the armor of God. He wants us to know that experientially, we have touched only the very frill, the very edge of this outpouring of the Spirit.

During the time Jesus was on the earth, the people cried out to him one day, but the disciples rebuked them. No, Jesus said, if these were to hold their peace, the very stones—from which he could make bread—would cry out in praise.

If we do not allow God to fill us with himself, he will choose somebody else. If we do not fall into line with the will of God, there will be somebody else who will. God is able to raise up others to carry out his bidding. May your prayer be as Isaiah's: "Here am I; send me" (Isaiah 6:8).

Going On with God

When we are baptized in the Holy Spirit, we must not allow speaking in tongues to entertain us. When you have accomplished one thing in the purpose of God for you, he will enlarge you and fit you for the next thing he wants you to do.

When I was baptized in the Holy Spirit, there was an unfolding of a new era of my life, and I passed into it and rejoiced in the fact of it. But the moment I reached that new era, God was ready with another ministry for me.

Too many people are concerned about what their appearance will be like in the glory. The chief thing is to realize within yourself a deeper manifestation of the power of God today than yesterday; that you experienced the mind of the Spirit more clearly today than you had the day before; that nothing comes between you and God to cloud your mind. You are to see a vision of the glory of God more today than yesterday, and to live in such a state of bliss that it is heavenly to live. Paul lived in that ecstasy because he got into a place where the Holy Spirit could enlarge him more and more.

I find that if I continually keep my mind upon God, he unfolds things to me, and if I obediently walk before God and keep my heart pure and clean and holy and right, he will always be lifting me higher than I have ever expected to be.

A Living Sacrifice

In Romans 12:1, Paul speaks about a certain place of commitment being reached—he speaks about an altar on which he had laid himself. "I beseech you therefore, brethren, by the mercies of God that ye present your bodies a living sacrifice, holy, acceptable unto God, which is your reasonable service."

When he had experienced the mercies of the Lord, he could do no other than make a presentation of his body on the altar, and it was always to be on the altar and never to be taken off.

Because Paul so lived in the Spirit, God put his mind into Paul's so that the apostle could write and speak as an oracle of the Holy Spirit. He wrote things that had never been in print before, things portraying the mind of God. We read them today and drink them in as a river, and come out of the Epistles clothed with mighty power—the power of God, himself.

How does it come? It comes when we are in a place low enough, and where God can pour in, pour in, pour in. Paul could say that not one thing God had spoken through him had failed. In Acts 16 and Romans 15, you will find that he accomplished the whole of what Jesus said he would accomplish, when he was reorganized, or filled, or in-filled by the mighty power of God.

God wants to do the same for you and for me, according to the gifts he has bestowed upon us.

꘎❥ ꘎❥ ꘎❥

Pressing Toward the Goal

Shall we stop short of what God says we ought to be? Shall we cease to come into line with the mind, which is always thinking for our best? Shall we cease to humble ourselves before him who took the way of the cross for us? Shall we cease to withhold ourselves from him who could weep over the doomed city, from the Lord Jesus Christ who "trod the wine press alone?" Shall we cease to give him our all?

What will it profit us if we hold back anything from him who gives us a thousand times more than ever he asks from us? In Hebrews 2, the Lord says he is going to bring many sons to glory. It means he is going to clothe them with his glory. Let that be your vision. If you have lost the vision, he is tender to those who cry to him. He never turns away from the broken heart, and those who seek him with a whole heart will find him (Jeremiah 29:13).

Today I feel that somehow my heart is very much enlarged, that my compassion for my Lord is intensified, that nothing is too hard. I feel there is a measure of grace given to the person who says, "I will go all the way with Jesus." What is that measure of grace? It is a girding with hopefulness in pressing forward to the goal that God would have us reach. There is a possibility that some who have sown the good seed of the Gospel might lose out. God forbid!

It is important that we do not forget our Lord's words: "Behold I come quickly: hold that fast which thou hast, that no man take thy crown" (Revelation 2:11).

Knowing God's Purpose

I have a Jesus who can speak the Word, and the thing is done. I have a Jesus indwelling me and vitalizing me with a faith that believes it is true. I have a Jesus within me who has never let me become faint-hearted or weary.

You must not forget that which the Holy Spirit puts into your heart as his purpose for you.

Our brethren are going out into the streets tonight, and I may be amongst them. They will be preaching, and they will say, "Every one who believeth can be saved." They will mean that everyone who believes can be healed. The same truth. They will emphasize it over and over again. They have no more right to emphasize that than I have a right to say, "He was wounded for our transgression, he was bruised for our iniquities: the chastisement of our peace was upon him; and with his stripes we are healed" (Isaiah 53:6).

Let us press on in faith to do God's will, and the outpouring, which we have longed for, will come. Cheer up; hold on; never let go of the vision. Be sure it is for you, just as much as for anybody else, and God will surely make it come to pass. Never look down, because then you will only see the ground and miss the vision. All blessings come from above; therefore keep your eye on Jesus. Never weary. If you do not fall out by the way, he will be with you to strengthen you in the way. Hallelujah!

-166-

Being Born of God

God wants us to be so built up in truth, righteousness, and the
life of God that every person we come in contact with knows,
of a truth, we are of God. And we who are of God can assure
our hearts before him, and we can have perfect confidence. We
must not look at the Word as only a written word. The Word is
a live fact to work in the human body living truths—changing it,
moving it till the person is a living fact of God's inheritance, till
God reigns in them. In conversation or activity, the believer is a
product of God.

Let us look at 1 John 1:1 for essential truths: "Whosoever believeth
that Jesus is the Christ is born of God; and everyone that loveth
him that begat loveth him also that is begotten of him."

What is the outcome of being born of God? God's life is God's
truth, God's walk, God's communion, fellowship, oneness, like-
mindedness. All that pertains to Almightiness, righteousness, and
truth comes forth from new birth. In it, through it, and by it, we
have a perfect regenerated position. Again, it is an impartation of
love and expression of himself, for God is love.

If you think back to when you first believed in your heart, you felt so
holy, you felt so loved that you were in a paradise of wonderment.
And for days and days, you had no desire for sin. Beloved, that
wonderful experience can be renewed day by day.

Overcoming the World

We want to be so established in God that nothing in this world will be able to move us from our perfect position. See how much God has for us in the world. God wants people who are mighty in the Spirit, who are full of power. God has great designs for man. He has determined by his power and his grace, through his Son, to bring many sons unto glory, clothed upon with the Holy One from Heaven.

God is jealous over us today. He longs for us to catch the breath of his Spirit! He longs for us to move in union with himself so that the Holy Spirit can breathe through our natural life and chasten it by his divine power, giving us a new faith, a new revelation of God. We see that if we are born of God, we can overcome the world: "And this is the victory that overcometh the world, even our faith. Who is he that overcometh the world but he that believeth that Jesus is the Son of God" (1 John 5:4, 5).

Now look at the book of Revelation for more on overcoming: "He that hath an ear, let him hear what the Spirit saith unto the churches; To him that overcometh will I give to eat of the tree of life, which is in the midst of the paradise of God" (Revelation 2:7). "And they overcame him [the devil] by the blood of the Lamb, and by the word of their testimony; and they loved not their lives unto the death" (Revelation 12:11).

It is most beautiful! We shall have to come into divine measurement, divine revelation. The possibilities are ours.

As Little Children

The first thing that God does with a newborn child is to keep him or her as a child. There are wonderful things for children. The difference between a child and the wise and prudent is this: the prudent person is too careful. The wise person knows too much. But the babies!

Look at God's spiritual babies—we have all been there. The spiritual child cannot dress itself, but God clothes it. He has a special raiment for children, white and beautiful. The babe cannot talk, but it is lovely to know that you will take no thought what you shall say (Matthew 10:19). The Holy Spirit can speak through you. He loves his children. Oh, how beautifully he looks after his children; how kind and good he is.

He that believes that Jesus is the Son of God overcomes the world, because Jesus is so holy and you become his habitation (1 John 5:4). Jesus is so sweet, his love passes all understanding. His wisdom passes all knowledge and therefore he comes to you with the wisdom of God and not of this world. He comes to you with peace, not as this world giveth. He comes to you with boundless blessing, with measure pressed down and running over. God is a rewarder of all who diligently seek him, for they that seek him shall lack no good thing (1 Thessalonians 4:12).

Surely, the Lord is not going to send you away empty. He wants to satisfy your longing soul with good things.

Loving God and One Another

I never forget when we had our first baby. While he slept in the cradle, my wife and I both went to him, and my wife would say, "I cannot bear to have him sleep any longer. I want him." And I remember waking the baby because she wanted him. "If ye then, being evil, know how to give good gifts unto your children, how much more shall your heavenly Father give the Holy Spirit to them that ask him?" (Luke 11:13). Ah, he is such a lovely Father.

One time I thought I had the Holy Spirit. Now I know the Holy Spirit has got me. There is a difference between our hanging on to God and God lifting us up. There is a difference between my having a desire and God's desire filling my soul. There is a difference between natural compassion and the compassion of Jesus that never fails. Human faith fails, but the faith of Jesus never fails.

Oh, beloved, I see through these glorious truths a new dawning: churches loving one another, all of one accord. Until that time comes, there will be deficiencies. "By this shall all men know that ye are my disciples, if ye have love one to another" (John 13:35). Love is the secret and center of the divine position. Where are your boundaries today? There are heights and depths and lengths and breadths to the love of God. The Word of God contains the principles of life. I live not, but another mightier than I liveth in me. The desires have gone into the desire of God.

Oh, how God loves his children!

A Faith That Cannot Be Denied

You ask what is the gift of faith. It is where God moves you to believe. Elijah was a man with passions like ours. The sins of the people were grieving the heart of God, and the whole house of Ahab was in an evil state. But God moved upon this man Elijah and gave him an inward cry: "There shall not be dew nor rain these years, but according to my word" (1 Kings 17:1). "And it rained not on the earth by the space of three years and six months" (James 5:17).

Oh, if we dared believe God! A man of like passions as we are stirred with Almightiness. "And he prayed again and the heaven gave rain, and the earth brought forth her fruit" (James 5:18).

Brother, sister, you are now in the robing room. God is adding another day for you to come into line, for you to lay aside everything that has hindered you so you can help others.

"Is any among you afflicted? Let him pray. Is any merry? Let him sing psalms. Is any sick among you? Let him call for the elders of the church; and let them pray over him, anointing him with oil in the name of the Lord: And the prayer of faith shall save the sick, and the Lord shall raise him up; and if he has committed sins, they shall be forgiven him. Confess your faults one to another, and pray one for another, that ye may be healed. The effectual fervent prayer of a righteous man availeth much" (James 5:13-16).

Do you want to touch God for faith that cannot be denied? I have learned this day if I dare put up my hands in faith, God will fill them. Come on, beloved, seek God and let us get a little touch of Heaven today.

Faith Is the Victory

Through faith we understand that the worlds were framed by the Word of God, so that things which are seen were not made of things which do appear (Hebrews 11:3).

You will notice that I keep coming back to the truth that faith is a reality, and God wants to bring us to the fact of it. He wants us to know that we have something greater than we can see or handle, because everything we can see and handle is going to pass away. The heavens are going to be wrapped up, and the earth will melt with fervent heat, but the Word of the Lord shall abide forever (Matthew 24:35).

God spoke the Word and made the world, and I want to impress upon you this wonderful Word, which made the world. I am saved by the incorruptible Word, the Word that made the world, and so my position by faith is to lay hold of the things which cannot be seen, and believe the things which cannot be understood.

Faith lives in a commanding position where you know God will work the miracle—if you dare to stand upon the Word.

> *Faith is the victory!*
> *Faith is the victory!*
> *Oh, glorious victory*
> *That overcomes the world.*
> *- John Henry Yates*

A Place of Command

Paul related his conversion many times over, and I believe it is good to rehearse what God has done for you. I have been privileged to be in many parts of the world, and have seen that God has arranged a plan for me. When it was time to leave home, I said to our people, "The Lord is moving me to go out through the States and Canada."

When the Lord told me to go, I prayed that he would provide money to support my family at home, provide money for my travels, and improve my memory.

Immediately money came from all over, and I said, "It is true God is sending me. I have already $250." I went to Liverpool, and a man said, "Here is $25 for you." When I boarded the ship, a poorly dressed woman gave me a red sugar bag; and when the ship sailed, I opened the bag and found $250.

But something else happened before I boarded the ship. A man gave me a book [diary] and said, "There is a page for every day in the year." The Lord said to me, "Put down everything that takes place in the month." I did so, and I had a memory like an encyclopedia. You see, I never learned geography, and God sent me all over the world to see it.

The Lord has a way of making you equal to living in a place of command in the power of the Holy Spirit so long as you have learned the lesson needed. God will teach you how to live.

Fire Burning in the Soul

Live in the Acts of the Apostles, and you will see every day some miracle wrought by the power of the living God. Do not fail to claim your holy position so that you will overcome the power of the devil. The best time you have is when you have the most difficult position. Sometimes the strangest things happen for the furtherance of the gospel.

One day I went to a Quakers' meeting, which are quiet and still. There was such a silence in that place that I was moved. You know it is of faith, and so I jumped up and spoke. I had the time of my life. All these Quakers came round me. They said, "You are the first man that we have ever seen in this place who was so quickly led by the Spirit." John says it is the unction of the Holy One, and you need no man to teach you—it is the Holy Spirit who teaches. It is simplicity itself.

> *Tis burning in my soul,*
> *Tis burning in my soul,*
> *The fire of heav'nly love is*
> *burning in my soul;*
> *The Holy Spirit came,*
> *All glory to his name!*
> *The fire of heavenly love*
> *is burning in my soul.*
> *- Delia T. White*

Always Ready

I always look for opportunities to witness for my Savior wherever I am. While I was on a ship, someone told me of entertainment they were planning and asked if I wanted to participate. When they told me they were planning a dance at the end, I told them to put me down for a song just before the dance. Then I began praying.

When the scheduled entertainment came and they had all done their pieces, my turn came. I went to the piano with my "Redemption Song." The pianist, a woman who was rather less than half dressed, saw the music and said, "I cannot play this kind of music." I said, "Be at peace, young lady, I have music and words inside." So I sang:

> *If I could only tell him as I know him,*
> *My Redeemer who has brightened all my way.*
> *If I could tell how precious is his presence,*
> *I am sure that you would make him yours today.*
> *Could I tell it. Could I tell it,*
> *How the sunshine of his presence lights my way,*
> *I would tell it, I would tell it.*
> *And I'm sure that you would make him yours today.*
> *- Author Unknown*

They did not have a dance, but they had a prayer meeting. They were weeping, and six young men were saved by the power of God in my cabin. Every day God saved people on that ship. "Preach the Word; be instant in season, out of season; reprove, rebuke, exhort with all longsuffering and doctrine" (2 Timothy 4:2).

⁊⇒ ⁊⇒ ⁊⇒

-175-

God Makes No Mistakes

I was at the Southampton train station on my way to Bournemouth [England]. When the train arrived, I got on. But I soon found that I had gotten into the wrong carriage. There was a man in the carriage, and I said to him, "I have been to Bournemouth before, but I do not seem to be on the way." "Where are you going?" he asked. "I am going to South Wales," I said, and then added, "Well, if I am wrong, I am right. I have never once been wrong in my life—only when I have been right."

I then turned to the man and asked, "What is the Lord Jesus Christ to you? He is my personal Friend and Savior." He replied, "I thank you not to speak to me about these things."

The train stopped, and I said to the porter, "Am I on the right train for Bournemouth? How many stops?" He answered, "Three."

I turned again to the man, "It has to be settled before I leave the train; you are going to hell." That man wished he had never met me. The train stopped, and I had to get out. I said, "What are you going to do?" He answered, "I will make him my own."

Beloved, if you believe in your heart, whatsoever you say will come to pass. If you believe in your heart (Mark 11:23).

Entering into His Rest

Today I believe that it is in the perfect will of God that you read some verses out of the fourth chapter of Hebrews. God wants us all to see in this chapter that we must not come short of that blessed rest. I am not speaking about the rest there is through being saved, although that is a very blessed rest. I am not speaking about the rest we have in the body when pain stops, nor of the rest when sanctification has worked in a wonderful way by the Blood and we have no sin. But God wants me to speak about the rest where you cease from your own works, and where the Holy Spirit begins to work in you and where you know that you are not your own, but absolutely possessed by God.

Beloved, I ask you to diligently follow me on these lines because there are so many people who are at unrest. I believe that God can bring us into a place of rest this day where we will cease from our own works, where we will cease from our own planning, where we will cease from our own human individuality, which so interferes with God's power within us. God wants to fill our body with himself—yes, to fill our body so full of himself, that we are **not**. It is then that God takes us into his plan, his pavilion, his wisdom, and the government shall be upon his shoulders.

Our Confidence Is in Christ

As believers, we have trusted in Christ toward God: "Not that we are sufficient of ourselves, to think anything as of ourselves, but our sufficiency is of God" (2 Corinthians 3:4, 5). Ah, it is lovely! Those verses are too deep to pass over. Here is a climax of exaltation that is so different from human exaltation. We want to get to a place where we are beyond trusting in ourselves.

Beloved, there is so much failure in self-assurances. We must never rest upon anything that is human. Our trust is in God, and God brings us into victory. When we have no confidence in ourselves, then our whole trust rests upon the authority of the mighty God. He has promised to be with us at all times, and to make the path straight, and to make a way through the mountains.

> *My hope is built on nothing less*
> *than Jesus' blood and righteousness;*
> *I dare not trust the sweetest frame*
> *but wholly lean on Jesus' name.*
> *– Edward Mote*

Our confidence can only be stayed on the one who never fails, the one who knows the end from the beginning. The day and night are alike to the man who rests completely in the will of God knowing that "All things work together for good to them that love God" (Romans 8:28).

The Sin of Unbelief

For the weapons of our warfare are not carnal, but mighty through
God to the pulling down of the strongholds; casting down
imaginations, and every thing that exalteth itself against the
knowledge of God, and bringing into captivity every thought to
the obedience of Christ (2 Corinthians 10:4, 5).

Now, the Holy Spirit will take the Word, making it powerful
in you till every evil thing that presents itself against the
obedience and fullness of Christ will absolutely wither away. I
want to show you the need of the baptism of the Holy Spirit, by
which you know there is such a thing as perfect rest, a perfect
Sabbath coming to your life. I want you to see Jesus. When he
lay asleep, filled with the Holy Ghost, the storm began to blow so
terribly and filled the ship with water. His disciples cried, "'Master,
carest thou not that we perish?' And he arose [filled with the Holy
Spirit] and rebuked the wind. He asked, "'Why are ye so fearful?'"
(Mark 4:38-40).

There remaineth a rest to the people of God. God wants you to
enter into that rest. "For he that is entered into his rest, he also
hath ceased from his own works, as God did from his. Let us
therefore labour to enter into that rest, lest any man fall after the
same example of unbelief" (Hebrews 4:10, 11).

Enter into rest, get filled with the Holy Spirit, and unbelief will depart.
When they entered in, they were safe from unbelief, and unbelief is
sin. It is the greatest sin, because it hinders you from all blessing.

Being God's Channel

L et me encourage you today that God is a God of encouragement. "Neither is there any creature that is not manifest in his sight: but all things are naked and opened to the eyes of him with whom we have to do" (Hebrews 4:13). No creature is hid from his sight. It is not your body, it is Christ clothing upon you within, and you have no spot. He looks at your nakedness, at your weaknesses, at your sorrow of heart.

He is looking into you right now, and what does he see? "Seeing then that we have a great high priest that is passed into the heavens, Jesus, the Son of God, let us hold fast our profession" (Hebrews 4:14). What is our profession? I have heard so many people testifying about their profession. Some said, "Thank God, I am healed." "Thank God he has saved me." "Thank God he has cleansed me." "Thank God he has baptized me with the Holy Spirit." That is my profession—is it yours? That is the profession of the Bible, and God wants to make it your profession.

You have to have a ***whole*** Christ, a ***full*** redemption, you have to be filled with the Holy Spirit, just a channel for him to flow through: Oh, the glorious liberty of the gospel of God's power.

> *Heaven has begun with me,*
> *I am happy, now, and free,*
> *Since the Comforter has come,*
> *Since the Comforter has come.*
> *- Author Unknown*

Possession of the Rest

If you turn to the Scriptures, you will find that the whole of Israel is a plan for us to see that God would have taken them on to many victories, but could not because of their unbelief. They were eligible for all the fullness of God, but Joshua and Caleb were the only two to enter the Promised Land. The reason these two went in was because they had another spirit. The Spirit was so mighty upon Joshua and Caleb when they went to spy out the land that they had no fear.

The Holy Spirit was upon them, giving them a dignity of reverence to God. There were ten other people sent out; they had not received the Spirit, and came back murmuring. If you get filled with the Spirit and go on with him (not remaining stationary like so many do), you will never murmur anymore. Why did the other ten spies murmur? What was it? They had no rest.

These ten people said, "We shall become prey to them, and our children shall be slain by them;" and God said through Moses, "Your children shall go in, and ye shall be shut out." It was unbelief that kept them out.

"There remaineth therefore a rest to the people of God" (Hebrews 4:9) and the people who enter into that rest cease

Sources

Material for the devotional readings in this book was selected and adapted from sermons that Smith Wigglesworth preached in various parts of the world. The sermon titles, publication names, publication dates, and numbers of the readings are given below. The published sermons are accessible at the Assemblies of God Archives, 1445 Boonville, Springfield, Missouri 65802; and The Donald Gee Centre for Pentecostal and Charismatic Research, Mattersey Hall, Mattersey, Doncaster DN10 5HD England.

The numbers below indicate which devotions use the material listed.

A Living Faith (*Triumphs of Faith*, Oakland, California, pages 6-8, January 1930); 4-7, 9, 43.

Christ in Us (tract, Good News Hall, North Melbourne, Australia, published in the 1920s); 2, 10, 11, 33, 34, 36, 37, 39, 40, 42, 43, 134.

The Appointed Hour—Life Out of Death (*Latter Rain Evangel*, Chicago, pages 2-6, June 1923); 10, 11, 12, 13, 14, 15, 17, 38, 41, 130.

Immersed in the Holy Ghost (*Triumphs of Faith*, Oakland, California, pages 113, 114, May 1921);12, 128, 129, 203.

The Abiding Spirit (tract, reprinted from *Good News* magazine, North Melbourne, Australia, published in the 1920s); 24, 26-29, 31, 54, 96.

Faith (tract published by Good News Hall, North Melbourne, Australia, 1920s; also reprinted in *Triumphs of Faith*, Oakland, California), pages 102-105, May 1925); 32, 52, 55-67, 99, 100.

Faith (*Triumphs of Faith*, Oakland, California, pages 246-248, November 1925); 53, 97.

The Baptism of the Holy Spirit (*Triumphs of Faith*, Oakland,

California, pages 124-128, June 1925); 33-37.

Believe! The Way to Overcome (*Triumphs of Faith*, Oakland, California, pages 156, 157, July 1927); 38, 39.

Love (*Triumphs of Faith*, Oakland, California, pages 30-33, February 1924); 40, 25, 133-135, 2, 138.

A Straightened Place Where God's Face Is Revealed (*Pentecostal Evangel*, Springfield, Missouri, pages 2, 3, January 9, 1926); 68-74.

The Pentecostal Power (*Pentecostal Evangel*, Springfield, Missouri, pages 6, 7, November 12, 1927); 75, 151.

Divine Life and Divine Health (*Confidence* magazine, Sunderland, England, pages 129, 131, 132, April-June 1924); 68-71.

Divine Revelation (*Redemption Tidings*, London, July 1925, pages 3-6); 1, 80-82, 84, 85, 3

Full of the Holy Ghost (*Pentecostal Evangel*, Springfield, Missouri, pages 1, 8, 9, May 28, 1932); 83, 109-114.

Epistles of Christ Manifesting His Glory (*Triumphs of Faith*, Oakland, California, pages 28-31, February 1929), 86-88, 90, 85.

Possession of the Rest (*Triumphs of Faith*, Oakland, California, pages 53-57, March 1925); 89, 176, 178-180.

Experiences Wrought Out by Humility (*Redemption Tidings*, London, England, pages 3, 4, June 8, 1945); 30, 92-95, 98, 177.

Filled With God (tract, reprinted from *Good News* magazine, North Melbourne, Australia, 1920s); 101-108 (102 includes excerpt from *Faith*).

Spiritual Gifts (*Triumphs of Faith*, Oakland, California, pages 248-252, November 1914); 115, 116, 117, 119, 120, 137, 154.

Our Great Need (*Confidence*, Sunderland, England, pages 84, 87, 90, November-December 1917); 118, 128, 142, 145, 148-150, 152, 153 (includes excerpt from *Possession of the Rest*), 155, 158, 160-165.

About the Gifts of the Spirit (*Pentecostal Evangel*, Springfield, Missouri, pages 1, 5, October 27, 1928); 121-124.

Glory and Virtue (*Triumphs of Faith*, Oakland, California, pages 105-107, 119, May 1923); 125-127, 129, 156 Ordination (tract, reprinted from *Good News* magazine, North Melbourne,

Australia, 1920s);139-141, 143, 144, 146, 147, 157, 159/
Overcoming (*Triumphs of Faith*, Oakland, California, pages 154-
156, July 1924); 166-170.

A Place of Command (*Revival News*, place and date unknown,
pages 3, 4; also published in the *Pentecostal Evangel*
Springfield, Missouri, December 30, 1939, pages 4, 11); 171-
175.

ADDITIONAL READING ON SMITH WIGGLESWORTH

Nearly sixty years after Smith Wigglesworth's death, a number of
books about him, or containing his sermons, are available. Although
some accounts might beg documentation, the discerning reader
will discover a wealth of inspiration in the following books either
compiled for Wigglesworth or that others wrote about him. With
the exception of Joyce Lee, Roberts Liardon, P. J. Madden, and
Wayne Warner, the authors/compilers were English and knew
Wigglesworth and heard him preach.

Cartwright, Desmond, *The Real Smith Wigglesworth* (Tonbridge,
Kent, England, Sovereign World, 2000). A biography that attempts
to set the record straight on several legends.

Frodsham, Stanley Howard, *Smith Wigglesworth, Apostle of Faith*
(Springfield, Missouri: Gospel Publishing House, 1948). Also
published by the Assemblies of God of Great Britain and Ireland in
1949. A biography written by his old friend and published the year
after Wigglesworth's death. Much of the material is Wigglesworth's
autobiography as told to Frodsham during a meeting in Riverside,
California.

Hacking, William, *Smith Wigglesworth Remembered* (Tulsa:
Harrison House, 1981). Published in 1972 as *Reminiscences of
Smith Wigglesworth*. A friend's focus on Wigglesworth's "Great
Challenge to Daring Faith."

Hibbert, Albert, *Smith Wigglesworth: The Secret of His Power*

(Tulsa: Harrison House, 1982). A friend's attempt at analyzing Wigglesworth's spiritual power.

Hywel-Davies, Jack, *The Life of Smith Wigglesworth* (Ann Arbor, Mich.: Servant Publications, 1987). A well-researched biography by an English minister and writer. This book was originally published by Hodder and Stoughton, London, as *Baptised by Fire* in 1987.

Liardon, Roberts, *Cry of the Spirit* (Laguna Hills, California: Roberts Liardon Ministry, 1991). A collection of fourteen sermons. Originally published by Harrison House, Tulsa, 1990.

Madden, P. J., *The Wigglesworth Standard, The Standard for God's End-time Army* (Springdale, Pennsylvania: Whittaker House, 1993). Six of Wigglesworth's sermons along with the author's annotations.

Stormont, George, *Wigglesworth, A Man who Walked With God* (Tulsa: Harrison House, 1989). A brief biography by a minister who knew Wigglesworth and who would often lecture about him.

Warner, Wayne, *The Anointing of His Spirit* (Ann Arbor, Mich.: Servant Publications, 1994). Twenty-nine sermons in four parts. Features additional information in *"The Man and His Message"* at the end of each sermon.

Warner, Wayne, and Lee, Joyce, *The Essential Smith Wigglesworth* (Venice, CA: Regal, Gospel Light, 1999). Here are 48 selected Wigglesworth sermons with photographs, time line, and 26 international narratives.

Whittaker, Colin C., *Seven Pentecostal Pioneers* (Springfield, Missouri: Gospel Publishing House, 1985). A former editor of *Redemption Tidings*, London, Whittaker has included a chapter on Wigglesworth: "Smith Wigglesworth, The Apostle of Faith." Originally published in England in 1983 by Edward England Books.

Wigglesworth, Smith, *Ever Increasing Faith*, (Springfield, Missouri:

Gospel Publishing House, 1924,1971). A book of eighteen sermons which Wigglesworth preached in Springfield, Missouri, and which were taken down in shorthand. The visit to Springfield followed successful meetings in Australia, New Zealand, and other countries.

Wigglesworth, Smith, *Faith That Prevails*, (Springfield, Missouri: Gospel Publishing House, 1938). Seven more sermons taken in shorthand and published in book form.

The SPIRIT-FILLED CLASSICS Collection

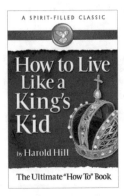

How to Live Like a King's Kid

by Harold Hill

The Ultimate "How To" Book

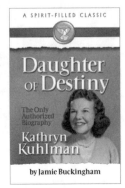

Daughter of Destiny

The Only Authorized Biography

Kathryn Kuhlman

by Jamie Buckingham

This inspiring collection includes biographies of famous men and women who operated in the Gifts of the Spirit as well as time-honored works by these influential figures.

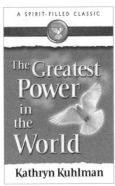

The Greatest Power in the World

Kathryn Kuhlman

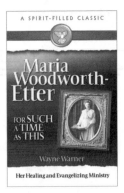

Maria Woodworth-Etter

FOR SUCH A TIME AS THIS

Wayne Warner

Her Healing and Evangelizing Ministry

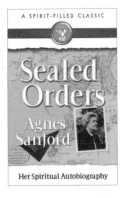

Sealed Orders

Agnes Sanford

Her Spiritual Autobiography

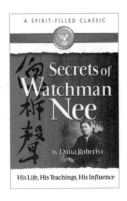

Secrets of Watchman Nee

by Dana Roberts

His Life, His Teachings, His Influence

The Holy Spirit & You

Over A Million Sold

Dennis & Rita Bennett

A Guide to the Spirit-Filled Life

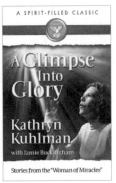

A Glimpse Into Glory

Kathryn Kuhlman

with Jamie Buckingham

Stories from the "Woman of Miracles"

AVAILABLE AT FINE CHRISTIAN BOOKSTORES